Explorations

An Interactive Approach to Reading

Alison Rice
Susan Stempleski

Hunter College of the City University of New York

COLLIER
MACMILLAN

Library of Congress Cataloging-in-Publication Data

Rice, Alison.
 Explorations: An interactive approach to reading.

 1. English language—Text-books for foreign
speakers. 2. Developmental reading. I. Stempleski,
Susan. II. Title.
PE1128.R448   1988   428.4'3   86-21810
ISBN 0-02-399760-5

Collier Macmillan Canada, Inc.

Editorial Production: Karen Davy
Cover, Design, and Illustrations: Anna Veltfort

Photo Credits: cover: Schecter Lee/ESTO; Devaney Stock Photos; © P. Moulu, Vandy Stadt/Photo Researchers; Ronald H. Cohn/The Gorilla Foundation.
page 1: Grandma Moses, *Checkered House*. Collection of IBM Corporation, Armonk, NY. Copyright © 1982, Grandma Moses Properties, New York. page 9: Metropolitan Museum of Art. page 10: Ronald H. Cohn/The Gorilla Foundation. page 20: top, Bettman Archives, Inc.; bottom, Paul Conklin/Monkmeyer Press Photo Service. page 30: Jil Robbins. page 42: top, Ken Lax; bottom, Linda Decker. page 43: top, Barbara Alper/Stock Boston; bottom, Gale Zucker/Stock Boston. page 48: Maggie Scarry. page 62: top, Len Rue, Jr./Leonard Rue Enterprises; bottom, Ira Kirschenbaum/Stock Boston. page 66: Stock Boston. page 70: top, Michael Weisbrot/Stock Boston; center, Gale Zucker/Stock Boston; bottom, Stock Boston. page 71: Patricia Hollander Gross/Stock Boston. page 78: Maggie Scarry. pages 80 and 87: Peter Marlow/Magnum. page 90: top left, Ellis Herwig/Stock Boston; top right, Vicky Horbovetz; center left, Michael Hayman/Stock Boston; center right, Jerry Howard/Stock Boston; bottom, George Malve/Stock Boston.

Grateful acknowledgment is given for the permission to use the following copyright material: (for page 32) "Face to Face in the Factories." *U.S. News & World Report,* 2 September 1985. (for page 34) "A Hard Day's Night." *Time,* 1 August 1983. (for page 44) "Active Dads See Rewards and Snags." *USA Today,* 7 November 1984. (for page 72) "TV as the New Fireplace." *Time,* 27 December 1982. (for page 86) "The Bird Men." *National Geographic,* August 1983.

First printing 1988

Printing: 1 2 3 4 5 6 7   Year: 8 9 0 1 2 3 4

Collier Macmillan
866 Third Avenue
New York, NY 10022

Printed in the U.S.A.

ISBN 0-02-399760-5

This book is dedicated to David, Daniel, and Amy Rice
and to John Stempleski and Helen Sutter.

Acknowledgments

We would like to express our appreciation to the many people whose help has made this book possible.

A very special thank you to Pamela McPartland, Director of the International English Language Institute at Hunter College, for her limitless encouragement and guidance, and for providing an atmosphere that inspires innovative teaching and creative materials development.

We are very grateful to our colleague, Tracey Forrest, who painstakingly read and field-tested the entire text. Her insightful comments and criticism were invaluable.

Many thanks to the fine editorial staff at Collier Macmillan: Mary Jane Peluso, whose enthusiasm and efficiency solved every problem; Maggie Scarry and Jil Robbins, for their interest and attention to detail; Larry Anger, Karen Peratt, and Carine Rostain for their support.

Thanks also to Karen Davy and Anna Veltfort for their tireless efforts.

We also appreciate the helpful comments of our reviewers: John Gibson, Ellen Clarkson, Rebecca Lemaitre, and Carol Pineiro.

Finally, a big thank you to all of our students and colleagues at the International English Language Institute and to our friends and families for their patience and encouragement.

Contents

Introduction

EXPLORATIONS is a textbook for high-beginning students in universities, language institutes, adult education programs, and high schools. The reading selections and learning activities presented are geared to adults and young adults studying English in the United States and abroad. The book may also be used by native speakers enrolled in developmental or remedial English programs.

The focus of EXPLORATIONS is on developing reading skills. As its title suggests, the text is interactive in its approach to language study. Students develop both their reading and oral skills through a wide variety of task-oriented and information-sharing activities for pairs and small groups of students. These include pre-reading discussions as well as post-reading comprehension exercises, paired interviews, and decision-making tasks. Underlying the approach is the conviction that students learn better if they are provided with interesting classroom activities in which they are personally involved.

Each chapter in EXPLORATIONS is based on a particular topic and contains the following learning activities:

- **Pre-Reading Group Discussion**

Centering on an illustration or questionnaire, pre-reading group discussion introduces the topic, motivates students to read the selections, lessens their fear of unfamiliar vocabulary, and provides opportunities for them to exchange ideas.

- **Main Reading Selection**

Based on topics of interest to adults and young adults, these passages are adapted, simplified versions of articles from English-language magazines and newspapers. Each is approximately 350 words long, and retains the stylistic and organizational format of its original. This helps students transfer reading skills to unsimplified material in the future.

• Further Reading Selection
Related to the topic of the main reading selection, secondary selections are more informal. They include newspaper clippings, advertisements, graphs, charts, letters, and brochures.

• Reading Skills Exercises
Skills such as predicting, finding the main idea, scanning, skimming, sequencing, organizing facts, and making inferences are taught through exercises and activities that actively involve the learner. Although each chapter contains exercises in these skills, the type of exercise varies widely throughout the text, thus maintaining student interest.

• Comprehension Activities
These are designed to guide and check students' understanding of what they have read. Comprehension activities include TRUE-FALSE–IT DOESN'T SAY questions, matching facts to diagrams or photographs, and decision-making tasks based on information contained in the reading selection. Outlining of factual information also teaches organization.

• Vocabulary Study
Vocabulary activities stress getting the meaning from context and include practice with synonyms and antonyms, word families, dictionary skills, cloze exercises, and making analogies.

• Wrap-up Conversational Activities
These activities allow students to share their thoughts and feelings about the topic of the chapter, and to find out more about each other. Many of these exercises are designed to improve crosscultural understanding by stimulating discussion of the similarities and differences between the students' cultures and that of the United States. Wrap-up activities include paired interviews as well as role-playing, problem-solving, and decision-making tasks.

The Grand Old Lady of

American Art

Pre-reading

WORK WITH A GROUP

1. Look at the painting by Grandma
   Moses. Talk about what is happening in
   the picture. Write down any vocabulary
   words that are new for you.

   _____

2. What can you learn about people's lives
   in the late 19th century from looking at
   the picture? List five things.

   EXAMPLE: *They still used horses for
   traveling.*

   _____

   _____

   _____

   _____

   _____

   Was life for those people easier or more
   difficult than it is now? Why?

3. Now look at the painting as art. This
   style of painting is called "primitive."
   Does it look like a child's painting to
   you? Why?
   Do you think Grandma Moses is a great
   artist? Do you like this painting? Why?

Read the story, "The Grand Old Lady of
American Art." What do you think the title
means?

The Grand Old Lady of American Art

Anna Mary Robertson Moses was 80 years old when she had her first one-woman exhibition. It was called "What a Farmwife Painted." It showed 34 small paintings of 19th-century country life. When Grandma Moses died 21 years later, she was world-famous. People called her the
5   "grand old lady of American art."

She was born in 1860 on a farm in upstate New York. Life was not easy for her as a young girl. She had nine brothers and sisters. She did not have much education. When she was 12, she went to work. She took a job as a hired girl. She went to live with an old couple and
10   did their cooking and housekeeping.

In 1887, Anna married Thomas Salmon Moses. He was a farmer. They had ten children, but five of them died when they were babies. The marriage lasted until Thomas died in 1927.

Eleven years after her husband died, she started to paint more.
15   She was in her seventies. She always liked drawing, but had been too busy to paint before. Now farm work was difficult for her. She needed something to keep her busy.

Grandma Moses had no art training. At first, she copied picture postcards and prints from newspapers and magazines. Later, she began
20   to paint original farm scenes that she remembered from her childhood. She chose these rural subjects to show how Americans used to live.

Her paintings, which she exhibited locally, attracted little attention until she was "discovered" by an art collector named Louis Caldor. He saw some of her paintings in a drugstore window in Hoosick Falls, New
25   York. Two years later, in 1940, she had her first one-woman exhibition in a gallery in New York City.

During the next twenty years, she painted more than a thousand paintings and had more than a hundred exhibitions in the United States and Europe. In 1950 alone, her paintings were exhibited in six European
30   capitals, including Amsterdam, Paris, and Vienna. By the time of her death, at the age of 101, she was the most famous painter in the United States. She was also the best loved. Like her paintings, Grandma Moses was simple, honest, and full of life.

1 Scanning

Read each question. Then look at "The Grand Old Lady of American Art" to find the answer as quickly as possible.

EXAMPLE: How many children did Grandma have? ___*10*___

1. How old was Grandma when she had her first exhibition? _____ years old

2. In what year was she born? _____

3. How old was she when she went to work? _____

4. When did Thomas Moses die? _____

5. How old was Grandma when she began to paint? _____

6. When did she have her first one-woman exhibition? _____

7. How many exhibitions did she have between 1940 and 1960? _____

8. About how many pictures did she paint? _____

9. In 1950, how many European capitals did she exhibit in? _____

10. How old was she when she died? _____ years old

2 Finding the Main Idea
WORK WITH A PARTNER

Choose the best answer.

1. "The Grand Old Lady of American Art" is about
   a) a painter that everyone loved.
   b) a painting of a rich old woman.
   c) a farmer who married a painter.

2. Grandma Moses began to paint when she was in her seventies because
   a) she wanted to become famous.
   b) she wanted to keep busy.
   c) her husband was dead.

3. People love her paintings because
   a) they look like a child's paintings.
   b) they show 19th-century American life in a colorful, lively way.
   c) if an old woman can paint, anyone can paint!

Decide if the statements are true (T) or false (F). Write the sentence from the story that supports your answer. If the article doesn't give the answer, write *It doesn't say*.

EXAMPLE: Grandma Moses had a long life. ___*T*___

She died when she was 101 years old.
_____

1. Grandma came from a small family. _____
_____

2. Grandma had an easy life. _____
_____

3. Grandma was married for 40 years. _____
_____

4. Grandma took art lessons. _____
_____

5. Grandma wanted people to know about old-time America. _____
_____

6. Louis Caldor first saw Grandma's paintings in a gallery. _____
_____

7. People around the world knew Grandma's paintings. _____
_____

8. Grandma was a good person. _____
_____

④ Vocabulary

1. GETTING THE MEANING FROM CONTEXT. Read each sentence and fill in the space with a word from the story. Look in the box if you need help.

1. New York State is very large. People who live in the southern part, near New York City, call the northern part " _____ ."

2. Grandma Moses didn't study art from a teacher or in art school. She didn't have any _____ in painting or drawing.

3. Do you own an _____ Grandma Moses painting? If you do, you're very lucky! Most people have copies or prints in art books.

4. Another name for the city is "an urban area." Another name for the countryside is "a _____ area."

5. A store that sells expensive paintings is a _____ .

6. Most artists want to have an _____ of their paintings, because they want people to see their paintings and buy them.

exhibition	original	training
gallery	rural	upstate

2. RECOGNIZING SYNONYMS. Find the words in the article that mean the same, or almost the same, as the words below.

EXAMPLE: line 3   pictures _paintings_

1. line 2   a wife who lives on a farm _____
2. line 4   very well-known _____
3. line 9   a young cleaning woman _____
4. line 12   very young children _____
5. line 15   making pictures with a pencil _____
6. line 18   drew something exactly like something else _____
7. line 20   the time when you're a child _____
8. line 26   a show of paintings _____
9. line 30   a city where the government meets _____
10. line 33 very active _____

5

THE

METROPOLITAN

MUSEUM OF

ART

6 *Scanning*

WORD GROUPS. Look at the reading about the Metropolitan Museum of Art.
Find the following groups of words.

EXAMPLE: Three artists: *Rembrandt, El Greco, and Manet*

1. Four continents: _____ , _____ , _____ , and
   _____

2. Three kinds of buildings: _____ , _____ , and
   _____

T here are many fine museums in New York, but the most famous is the Metropolitan Museum of Art. It is also the biggest museum in New York. There are more than 3 million works of art in the Metropolitan. It is so big that it is a good idea to try to see only one or two parts during each visit. 5

You can see art from all over the world at the Metropolitan. The Egyptian collection is on the main floor. It contains jewelry and mummies from ancient Egypt. There is also an ancient Egyptian temple, the Temple of Dendur. In the Greek and Roman collections, you can see statues, gold, silver, glass, and coins. The museum also has interesting collections of art 10 from North, Central, and South America, Africa, and Asia, including a copy of a Chinese scholar's house and garden!

There are more than 3,000 paintings by European artists in the Metropolitan. They date from 1200 to 1900. Most are by Flemish, Dutch, French, and Italian artists. But there are also fine paintings by British and 15 Spanish painters. Rembrandt's *Self-Portrait*, Manet's *The Spanish Singer*, and El Greco's *View of Toledo* are examples of paintings in the European collection.

If you are interested in music, you will enjoy the collection of musical instruments. It contains ancient and modern instruments from six continents. There are more than 4,000 different instruments in the collection, 20 but only 800 of them are on display at one time.

Many people like to start their visit in the American Wing. There you can see paintings and statues by American artists. You can also see examples of furniture, silver, and glass. There is even a complete living room on display! 25

The museum is really a collection of collections. There is so much to see at the Met that many people return again and again.

3. Six European nationalities: _____ , _____ ,

_____ , _____ , _____ , and _____

4. Two metals: _____ and _____

5. Seven kinds of collections in the museum that are *not* paintings: _____ ,

_____ , _____ , _____ , _____ ,

_____ , and _____

Choose the best answer.

1. The main idea of paragraph 1 is
   a) there are many fine museums in New York.
   b) the Metropolitan is the biggest museum in New York.
   c) it's a good idea to visit only one or two parts of the Metropolitan on one day.

2. The main idea of paragraph 2 is
   a) the Metropolitan has art from the Americas, Africa, and the Far East.
   b) the Egyptian collection is on the main floor.
   c) the Metropolitan has art from all over the world.

3. The main idea of paragraph 3 is
   a) there is a painting by Rembrandt in the Metropolitan.
   b) the Metropolitan has more than 3,000 European paintings.
   c) there are some fine British and Spanish painters.

4. Another title you can use for this article is
   a) "The Museums of New York."
   b) "European Art at the Metropolitan Museum."
   c) "The Biggest Museum in New York."

8 *What Does It Mean?*

PRONOUN REFERENCE. Connect the circled pronouns with the words they refer to.

The Metropolitan Museum of Art is the most famous museum in New York. (It) is also the biggest. (It) has more than 3 million works of art. (They) are from all over the world. Most of (them) are paintings and sculptures, but not all. Some of (them) were not originally art. For example, there are coins, furniture, and glassware. There is also a small Egyptian temple. (This) was given to the museum by the Egyptians when (they) built the Aswan Dam because (it) was going to be under water.

9 Problem-Solving

WORK WITH A GROUP

A VISIT TO THE MET. Plan an afternoon visit to the Metropolitan Museum of Art. You have time to visit only two parts of the museum. Study the floor plan carefully. Tell the group where *you* would like to go and listen to your friends' ideas.

What two parts will you visit?

1. _____

   Why? _____

2. _____

   Why? _____

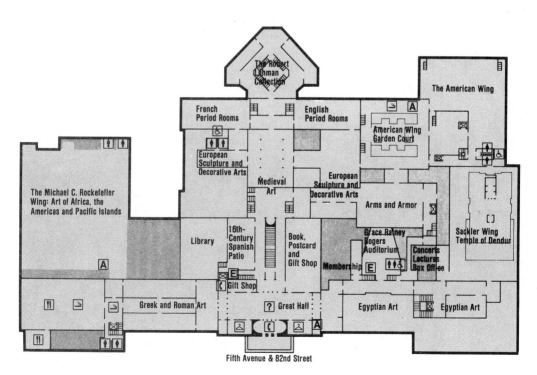

The Metropolitan Museum of Art

A Talking Gorilla

CHAPTER 2

Pre-reading

WORK WITH A PARTNER

1. Look at the pictures of Koko at the
   Gorilla Foundation. Tell what you see
   in the pictures. Write down any
   vocabulary words that are new for you.

   _____

2. What do you know about gorillas? Are
   the following statements true or false?

   a. Gorillas are bigger than people. _____

   b. Gorillas can speak to each other in
      English. _____

   c. Gorillas are stupid animals. _____

   d. Gorillas know the difference between
      the past and the future. _____

   e. Gorillas can spell. _____

Read the article, "A Talking Gorilla." Then
answer the true/false questions again. See
if your answers are the same. Which
question wasn't answered in the article?

A Talking Gorilla

Koko is a female gorilla. She lives at the Gorilla Foundation in California. Koko is not an ordinary gorilla. She can "talk." Koko knows and uses more than 500 words in sign language—the language of deaf people.

5   In the 1960s, researchers taught chimpanzees to understand and use sign language. Washoe, a female chimpanzee, learned 132 signs in four years. Most people, however, did not believe that gorillas could learn sign language. They thought that gorillas were not as smart as chimpanzees.

10   In 1972, Dr. Francine "Penny" Patterson started to teach sign language to Koko. The gorilla was one year old at the time. After only 36 months, Koko could use 184 signs! Her sign language vocabulary included words like *airplane, lollipop, friend,* and *stethoscope*.

      Koko continued to learn fast. Today she can do many of the
15 same things that humans can do with language. She can ask and answer questions. She can tell when she feels happy or sad. She can talk about the past or the future. She can insult people. She can even tell lies!

      Dr. Patterson, a psychologist, has tested Koko's IQ. Her
20 scores are between 85 and 95—a little below the IQ of an average human child. Testing Koko's IQ is not easy. Some test questions are unfair to gorillas. For example, Koko was asked to choose between a house or a tree for shelter from the rain. Koko naturally chose the tree. The answer was marked wrong.

25   Dr. Patterson also uses spoken language with Koko. Because of this, Koko can understand hundreds of spoken words. Koko herself cannot use spoken language, but she loves to listen to people's conversations. Researchers at the Gorilla Foundation have to spell out words like *c-a-n-d-y* and *g-u-m* when Koko is nearby.

30   People used to think that only humans could use language. It is true that gorillas cannot use their lips and tongues to speak, but they can communicate with people in other ways. Koko has taught us that gorillas are smart—at least as smart as chimpanzees. And we have a lot more to learn from her.

1 Scanning

Read each question. Then look at "A Talking Gorilla" to find the answer as quickly as possible.

1. How many signs did Washoe learn?

   a) 123   b) 132   c) 321

2. When did Dr. Patterson begin to teach Koko?

   a) in 1972   b) in the 1960s   c) in 1927

3. How old was Koko when she began to study sign language?

   a) 36 months   b) one year   c) four years

4. How high is Koko's IQ?

   a) 65–75   b) 75–85   c) 85–95

5. How many spoken words does Koko understand?

   a) under 100   b) between 100 and 200 c) more than 500

2 Finding the Main Idea
WORK WITH A PARTNER

Choose the best answer.

1. The main idea of paragraph 1 is
   a) Koko lives in California.
   b) Koko the gorilla can use sign language.
   c) sign language is used by deaf people.

2. The main idea of paragraph 4 is
   a) Koko uses language the same way that people do.
   b) Koko likes to tell lies.
   c) Koko is a good language learner.

3. The main idea of paragraph 5 is
   a) Koko is pretty smart.
   b) human IQ tests aren't made for gorillas.
   c) it's difficult to test Koko's IQ.

4. The main idea of the last paragraph is
   a) gorillas can't use their lips and tongues to speak.
   b) we can learn more from research with gorillas.
   c) gorillas are as smart as chimpanzees.

13

1. TRUE OR FALSE? Decide if the statements are true (T) or false (F). Write the sentence from the story that supports your answer. If the article doesn't give the answer, write *It doesn't say*.

EXAMPLE: Koko lives in Africa. ___F___

She lives at the Gorilla Foundation in California.

1. Koko isn't a person. _____

_____

2. Koko has a large vocabulary. _____

_____

3. Scientists taught sign language to chimpanzees before 1970. _____

_____

4. Koko learned 36 signs in three years. _____

_____

5. Dr. Patterson's nickname is ''Penny.'' _____

_____

6. Koko is usually polite and honest. _____

_____

7. Dr. Patterson is a medical doctor. _____

_____

8. Koko can understand only a few words of spoken English. _____

_____

9. Candy is good for gorillas. _____

_____

10. We know everything about Koko. _____

_____

2. MAKING INFERENCES. Read each sentence and decide which answer is correct. Sometimes you have to read ''between the lines.'' Explain your answer.

14

EXAMPLE: Koko is a (better) language learner than Washoe.
worse

(Koko learned 184 signs in three years; Washoe learned only 132 signs in four years.)

1. Koko likes / doesn't like to eat candy.

2. Koko is a baby gorilla. / an adult gorilla.

3. Koko has / doesn't have an understanding of time.

4. It's easy / It's difficult to make an IQ test for a gorilla.

5. Gorillas are smarter than / almost as smart as average human children.

4 Vocabulary

WORD FORMS. Choose the form of the word that completes each sentence.

1. insults   insulting
   noun   adjective

   a. Koko told the visitor that he was stupid and ugly. These are her biggest

   _____ .

   b. She usually says _____ things when she's angry.

2. research   researcher
   noun   noun

   a. Dr. Patterson is a _____ at the Gorilla Foundation.

   b. _____ has taught us that gorillas can learn language.

3. speak   spoken
   verb   adjective

   a. Gorillas can't _____ English.

   b. They can't learn _____ language, but they can learn sign language.

4. true   truthfully
   adjective   adverb

   a. The information about Koko in this article is _____ .

   b. Do you always answer questions _____ ?

15

Further Reading

An Interview with Dr. Patterson

A reporter, Amy Daniel, is interviewing Dr. Penny Patterson, the Director of the Gorilla Foundation, about Koko, a talking gorilla.

Amy: Most people think that gorillas are stupid and cruel man-killers. Is that true?

Dr. Patterson: Not at all! Our experience with Koko has taught us that gorillas are bright—intelligent enough to learn sign language. And they can also be gentle. In fact, they have many of the same feelings 5 that people have.

Amy: Can you give me an example?

Dr. Patterson: Sure. Do you know about Koko's love for cats? Well, one of her favorite stories is "The Three Little Kittens." She likes me to read it to her a lot. One day, she told me that she wanted a pet 10 cat.

Amy: How did she do that?

Dr. Patterson: She made the sign for *cat*. She pulled two fingers across her face—like cat's whiskers. I bought her a toy cat, but she wasn't happy with it. She acted like a real baby—refused to play with 15 it, and just sat and pouted.

Amy: Did you buy her a kitten?

Dr. Patterson: Well, I didn't, but later someone brought three baby kittens to the Gorilla Foundation. When Koko saw them, it was love at first sight. She made the sign that says "love that" and pointed 20 to the kittens. She chose a gray male kitten with no tail for her pet, and named him "All Ball."

Amy: Was she rough with him? Did she hurt him?

Dr. Patterson: Oh, no! She was very gentle. She held him the way that mother gorillas hold their babies. She dressed him the way that children 25 dress their pets. All Ball sometimes hurt Koko, but she never hurt him.

Amy: I read about All Ball. Wasn't he killed by a car?

Dr. Patterson: Yes, it was horrible. He ran out into traffic. When we told Koko the news, she was silent for about ten minutes. Then she 30 began to cry—not with tears but with crying sounds. That's when I really understood that gorillas have feelings.

Amy: Does the story have a happy ending?

Dr. Patterson: Well, a warm one, anyway. Newspapers and television stations from around the world told the story of Koko and her kitten. 35 Hundreds of people, from as far away as Italy and Japan, called or wrote to the Gorilla Foundation. They wanted to give Koko a new pet. Finally, she chose another kitten. This one is orange, and like All Ball, he doesn't have a tail.

6 Vocabulary

DICTIONARY DEFINITIONS. Match the correct meaning with the sentence.

EXAMPLE: *smart* = a) clever, intelligent
b) fashionable, elegant

___*a*___ He was *smart* enough to get an A on his English exam.
___*b*___ Her clothes are always very *smart*.

1. *feel* = a) to experience an emotion
b) to examine by touching

_____ *Feel* the coffee pot to see if it's hot.
_____ He *feels* happy because he's in love.

2. *act* = a) to behave
b) to perform

_____ The young man *acted* in his first movie.
_____ The child *acted* very badly in the restaurant.

3. *bright* = a) strong; easily seen
b) intelligent

_____ That child is *bright*—he can read the *New York Times*.
_____ Her dress is *bright* red.

4. *sign* = a) a board with written information on it
b) to write one's name

_____ The *sign* said "No Parking."
_____ Will you please *sign* this check?

5. *pet* = a) to touch gently
b) an animal kept as a friend

_____ The children wanted a dog for a *pet*.
_____ Don't *pet* the lion.

6. *rough* = a) acting in a way that can hurt
b) not smooth

_____ The boy was sometimes *rough* with his little sister.
_____ The sweater was made of cheap, *rough* wool.

7. *lie* = a) to say something untrue
b) to rest one's body

_____ Don't *lie* to me! I know you ate the cake.
_____ The cat likes to *lie* on the sofa.

17

7 What Does It Mean?

PRONOUN REFERENCE. **Connect the circled pronouns with the words they refer to.**

Koko is a female gorilla. (She) lives at the Gorilla Foundation. (It's) a research institute in California. (There) (she) studies sign language with (her) teacher, Penny Patterson. Koko can't speak, but (she) can understand spoken language. Researchers have to be careful when (they're) near (her) . (They) must spell out words like *candy* or *gum* if (they) don't want Koko to ask for (some)

Write your partner's answers to the questions in the questionnaire.

PETS

Do you like or dislike animals? _____

Did you have a pet when you were a child? _____

Do you have a pet now? _____

  If yes, what kind of animal is it? _____

  What does it look like? _____

  What is its name? _____

Do many families in your country have pets? _____

  If yes, which animal is the most popular pet? _____

  If no, why don't they have pets? _____

Do you think that children should have pets? _____

  Why or why not? _____

Before you read about Koko, did you think that gorillas were intelligent animals? _____

What other animals do you think are intelligent? _____

Have you ever had a bad experience with an animal? _____
  If yes, tell me about it.

Thanksgiving—Then and Now

CHAPTER 3

Pre-reading

WORK WITH A GROUP

1. Look at the pictures of "Thanksgiving Then" and "Thanksgiving Now."
   Talk about what is happening in the pictures. Write down any vocabulary
   words that are new for you.

   _____

2. Which questions can you answer from looking at the pictures? Tell your
   group a reason for your answers.

   a. Is Thanksgiving a new holiday? _____

   b. Is it a family day? _____

   c. What do people eat on this day? _____

   d. What season (winter, spring, summer, fall) is Thanksgiving in? _____

   e. Why do people celebrate Thanksgiving? _____

   The next article is "Thanksgiving—Then and Now."   Check (✔) the things you think
   this article will talk about.

   ☐ Old and new ways of celebrating Thanksgiving
   ☐ The history of the holiday
   ☐ Reasons why Americans celebrate Thanksgiving
   ☐ All of these

21

Thanksgiving
Then and Now

Americans celebrate Thanksgiving Day on the fourth Thursday of November. It is one of the oldest American holidays. On Thanksgiving Day, Americans remember the Pilgrims—a small group of people who came to America more than 350 years ago.

5   The Pilgrims wanted to practice religion in their own way. The government of England did not permit this, so the Pilgrims left England. In September 1620, 102 of them got on a ship and sailed to America. Their ship was named the *Mayflower*.

    The voyage was long and hard. The ship was small and crowded. Many
10 Pilgrims became sick. Some of them died. After 66 days at sea, the *Mayflower* landed.

    The Pilgrims named the place where they landed Plymouth. They started to build houses there, but winter came very soon. They were not ready for the cold. They did not have enough warm clothing. They did not
15 have enough food. Half of them died that winter.

    At last, spring came. Some friendly Indians taught the Pilgrims how to plant new vegetables—beans, corn, and pumpkins. The Indians taught them how to hunt too.

    During the summer of 1621, their crops grew. In the fall, the Pilgrims
20 had a big harvest. They wanted to give thanks for the food, so they had a big feast. They invited their Indian friends.

    The first Thanksgiving celebration lasted three days. There was plenty of food to eat. There was turkey with nuts, beans, cornbread, and a sauce made from cranberries. For dessert, there was pumpkin pie. During the cele-
25 bration, the Indians and the Pilgrims played games together.

    In the United States today, Thanksgiving is a lot like the first Thanksgiving in Plymouth. Friends and families get together for a big dinner. They eat the same food that the Pilgrims and Indians ate in 1621. They often watch a football game in the morning or afternoon. In some cities, like New York and
30 Philadelphia, there are big Thanksgiving Day parades. For modern Americans, Thanksgiving Day is also a day for giving thanks for the good things they have enjoyed during the year.

1 Scanning

Read each question. Then look at "Thanksgiving—Then and Now" to find the answer as quickly as possible.

EXAMPLE: When did the Pilgrims leave England? *in 1620*

1. When do modern Americans celebrate Thanksgiving? _____

2. Who do Americans remember on this day? _____

3. How many Pilgrims left England? _____

4. What was the name of their ship? _____

5. How many days were they at sea? _____

6. What did they name the place where they landed? _____

7. What vegetables did they plant? _____

8. When was the first Thanksgiving? _____

9. How long was the celebration? _____

10. What did they eat for dessert? _____

2 Choosing a Different Title
WORK WITH A PARTNER

The title of the last article is "Thanksgiving—Then and Now." Look at the list of other titles below. Find four more that you think are also good. Number them, starting with the one you think is the best.

a) ____ Pilgrims, Pumpkins, and Parades
b) ____ The First Thanksgiving
c) ____ The Thanksgiving Table
d) ____ An Old American Holiday
e) ____ Thanksgiving: Why and How We Celebrate
f) ____ The Story of the Pilgrims
g) ____ Indians and Pilgrims
h) ____ A Trip to America
i) ____ Religion in England
j) ____ The Fourth Thursday in November

What is wrong with the other titles?

3 *Finding the Main Idea*

WORK WITH A PARTNER

Choose the best answer.

1. The main idea of paragraph 1 is
   a) Thanksgiving is an old American holiday.
   b) Thanksgiving comes on the fourth Thursday in November.
   c) the Pilgrims came to America over 350 years ago.

2. The main idea of paragraph 2 is
   a) the government of England didn't permit freedom of religion.
   b) the Pilgrims sailed to America on the *Mayflower*.
   c) the Pilgrims left England because they wanted religious freedom.

3. The main idea of paragraph 3 is
   a) some Pilgrims died during the voyage.
   b) the voyage was long and hard.
   c) the *Mayflower* was a small ship.

4. The main idea of paragraph 4 is
   a) the Pilgrims gave the name Plymouth to their landing place.
   b) winters in Plymouth are very cold.
   c) the Pilgrims had a very hard winter.

5. The main idea of paragraph 5 is
   a) beans, corn, and pumpkins are vegetables.
   b) Indians knew how to plant and hunt.
   c) Indians taught the Pilgrims how to plant and hunt.

6. The main idea of paragraph 6 is
   a) the Pilgrims invited the Indians to their feast.
   b) the Pilgrims had a big feast to give thanks for their harvest.
   c) the Pilgrims grew crops during the summer of 1621.

7. The main idea of paragraph 7 is
   a) turkey was served at the first Thanksgiving.
   b) Indians and Pilgrims enjoyed games together.
   c) the Pilgrims had a lot to eat at the first Thanksgiving.

8. The main idea of paragraph 8 is
   a) Thanksgiving celebrations in the United States today are similar to the first Thanksgiving.
   b) on Thanksgiving Day, Americans eat the same kinds of food that the Pilgrims ate at the first Thanksgiving.
   c) there are big Thanksgiving Day parades in New York and Philadelphia.

24

4 Comprehension

WORK WITH A PARTNER

1. TRUE OR FALSE? Decide if the statements are true (T) or false (F). Write the sentence from the story that supports your answer. If the article doesn't give the answer, write *It doesn't say.*

EXAMPLE: The Pilgrims' voyage to America was short and easy. ___*F*___
The voyage was long and hard.
_____

1. The Pilgrims' way of religion was the same as other people's in England. _____
_____

2. Everyone on the ship stayed healthy. _____
_____

3. The Pilgrims landed at Plymouth in November. _____
_____

4. The Pilgrims didn't eat beans, corn, and pumpkins in England. _____
_____

5. All of the Indians near Plymouth were friendly. _____
_____

6. The Pilgrim women cooked enough food for a party that lasted three days. _____
_____

7. Thanksgiving today is a family celebration. _____
_____

8. Today's celebration is very different from the first Thanksgiving. _____
_____

9. Modern Americans remember to be thankful on Thanksgiving. _____
_____

2. MAKING INFERENCES.   Read each sentence and decide which answer is correct.   Explain why.

1. Thanksgiving is $\begin{matrix} \text{always} \\ \text{usually} \end{matrix}$ the last Thursday in November.

2. The king of England $\begin{matrix} \text{liked} \\ \text{didn't like} \end{matrix}$ the Pilgrims' way of religion.

3. The Pilgrims $\begin{matrix} \text{enjoyed} \\ \text{didn't enjoy} \end{matrix}$ their voyage to America.

4. $\begin{matrix} \text{More} \\ \text{Fewer} \end{matrix}$ than 40 Pilgrims died before the first summer.

5. In England, the Pilgrims probably $\begin{matrix} \text{were} \\ \text{weren't} \end{matrix}$ farmers.

6. Massachusetts was $\begin{matrix} \text{warmer} \\ \text{colder} \end{matrix}$ than the Pilgrims had expected.

7. The Indians near Plymouth $\begin{matrix} \text{were} \\ \text{weren't} \end{matrix}$ afraid of the Pilgrims.

8. Modern Americans eat $\begin{matrix} \text{a lot} \\ \text{very little} \end{matrix}$ on Thanksgiving.

⑤ *Finding the Facts*

Answer each question.   Reread the article "Thanksgiving—Then and Now" if you don't remember the information.

1. Describe the Pilgrims' voyage on the *Mayflower*.

   a. *It was long—they were at sea for 66 days.* _____

   b. _____

   c. _____

   d. _____

2. What problems did the Pilgrims have during their first winter in Plymouth?

   a. _____

   b. _____

   c. _____

3. How is today's Thanksgiving the same as the first one?

a. _____

b. _____

c. _____

6 *Vocabulary*

1. GETTING THE MEANING FROM CONTEXT. Read each sentence. Find the word or phrase that is a definition or synonym for the underlined word in the sentence.

1. The Pilgrims left England because they wanted to practice religion in their own way. For example, they didn't want music in their churches.

a) a sport   b) a way of government   c) a belief in God or gods

2. The Pilgrims learned how to grow corn and pumpkins. English farmers didn't plant these crops.

a) food plants   b) flowers   c) short haircuts

3. Independence Day, Thanksgiving, and New Year's Day are national holidays in the United States.

a) religious days   b) days when no one works   c) days to eat a lot

4. Most Americans eat apple pie or pumpkin pie for dessert on Thanksgiving.

a) the main dish in a meal   b) something sweet at the end of a meal
c) fruit

5. Thousands of people come to see the Thanksgiving parade in New York. They hear music and see clowns and people in beautiful costumes.

a) dancing in the street   b) a line of people and marching bands walking
in the street   c) a party

WORD FORMS

2. Choose the form of the word that completes each sentence.

1. celebrate   celebration
       verb   noun
   a. Americans _____ Thanksgiving on the fourth Thursday of November.

   b. The best part of the _____ is eating turkey and pumpkin pie.

2. hunt   hunter
       verb   noun
   a. The Indians taught the Pilgrims how to _____ wild turkeys and deer.

   b. A person who chases wild animals for sport is a _____ .

3. religious   religion
       adjective   noun
   a. The Pilgrims wanted to practice their own way of _____ .

   b. In fact, they were more _____ than most other English people in 1620.

4. sailed   sailing
       verb   adjective
   a. The *Mayflower* was a _____ ship.

   b. The Pilgrims _____ for 66 days.

3. Fill in the word-form chart. The forms in Exercise 2 will help you. You may also use your dictionary.

NOUN	VERB	ADJECTIVE	ADVERB
	celebrate		X
hunter			X
	X	religious	
	sail		X

The Pilgrims served cranberry sauce at the first Thanksgiving celebration. Like the Pilgrims, modern Americans eat their Thanksgiving turkey with cranberry sauce too. Do you want to know how to make it? Read this easy recipe and find out.

Cranberry Sauce

4 cups (950 ml.) cranberries
1 cup water
2 cups granulated (white) sugar
Dash of salt

1. Wash the cranberries.
2. Put the cranberries and water in a saucepan.
3. Bring to a boil.
4. Cover the pan.
5. Cook for six to eight minutes.
6. Remove the mixture from the heat.
7. Stir in the sugar and salt.
8. Mix thoroughly.
9. Chill.
10. Serve with turkey.

Makes 2 pints (1 liter)

Match the steps in the recipe with the pictures. Write the number of each step under the picture.

_____ _____ _1_

_____ _____ _____

_____ _____ _____

Scanning

Read each question. Then look at the recipe to find the answer as quickly as possible.

1. How much sauce will this recipe make? _____

2. How many ingredients are in the recipe? _____

3. How many ingredients are liquid? _____

4. What is the first thing you do with the cranberries? _____

5. How long do you cook the sauce? _____

10 *Questionnaire*

WORK WITH A PARTNER

Write your partner's answers to the questions in the questionnaire.

HOLIDAYS

What country are you from? _____

What is your favorite national holiday? _____

When is it? _____

What is the reason for this holiday? _____

Who are you usually with on this day? _____

What do you usually do? _____

Are there traditional foods for this day? What are they? _____

_____

How did you spend this day last year? _____

Can you tell me anything else that is interesting or unusual about this holiday? _____

Tell the class something interesting that you learned about your partner's holiday.

A Day in the Life of Kotaro Nohmura

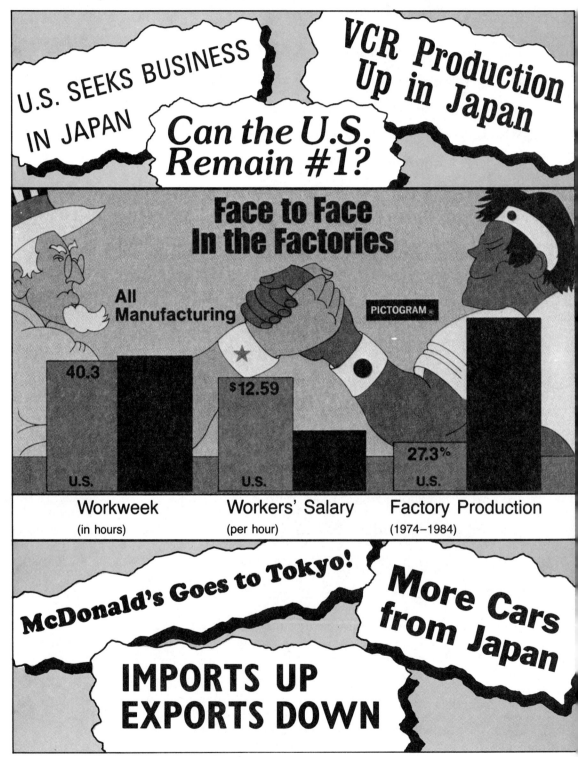

Pre-reading

WORK WITH A GROUP

1. **Look at the graphs in "Face to Face in the Factories." Are the following statements true or false?**

   a. Factory workers in Japan earn less per hour than in the United States. _____

   b. American factory output didn't grow between 1974 and 1984. _____

   c. In ten years, Japan's factory production doubled. _____

   d. American factory workers work about eight hours a day. _____

2. **What do the headlines, graphs, and picture tell you about American–Japanese business in the 1980s? List five facts.**

   a. _____

   b. _____

   c. _____

   d. _____

   e. _____

3. **What other facts do you know about the Japanese way of doing business?**

The next article, "A Day in the Life of Kotaro Nohmura," talks about a young, successful Japanese executive. As you read, compare his workday with that of a businessperson in your country.

A Day
in the
Life of
KOTARO
NOHMURA

When Kotaro Nohmura, an executive of an Osaka tent manufacturer, arrives home from work, it is almost midnight. He takes a quick look at his children.
5 They are asleep, exactly as they were when he left at 7:30 that morning. This is usually the only contact Nohmura (37) has with his two sons (7 and 4

months) and two daughters (5 and 9) during the week. Like most Japanese 10 executives, his day starts early and ends late.

Nohmura earns $51,000 a year before taxes. He and his family live in a four-room apartment outside the city 15 of Kobe. Six days a week, he gets up at 7:00 and eats a Western-style breakfast prepared by his 32-year-old wife, Sanae. Then he drives 40 minutes to his office in a busy section of Osaka. 20

Nohmura spends most of his morning in his tiny office. He likes his small space because he doesn't have to stand up to get what he needs. There he writes reports and talks about tent 25 designs with engineers. He seldom goes to business lunches. He usually has a quick bowl of noodles at a nearby restaurant.

In the afternoon, he visits local 30 customers and stops in at the factory. He usually leaves his office at about 5:30, but his work is not finished. For example, on a typical evening recently, he went to a meeting at a business- 35 men's club. After the meeting, he took two important clients to an elegant restaurant ($110 a person). They sat on cushions on the floor and ate a 12-course meal that included soup, 40 sashimi, and tempura. Next, the group went to a Western-style nightclub. There a hostess served them whiskey and brandy. They stayed there until after 11:00 P.M. The bill was $360. 45 Nohmura doesn't like entertaining, but it is an important part of doing business in Japan.

When Nohmura returned home, his wife met him at the door. They had 50 a cup of green tea together, and talked about the coming Sunday. The family was going to go to the beach for a picnic. Sunday is Nohmura's one day off.

Scanning

Read each number in the left column. Then look at the article, "A Day in the Life of Kotaro Nohmura," to find what it refers to. Write that fact on the right.

EXAMPLE: 37 *Kotaro Nohmura's age*

1. 5 and 9 _____

2. $51,000 _____

3. six _____

4. 40 _____

5. 5:30 _____

6. $110 _____

7. 12 _____

8. 11:00 _____

9. $360 _____

10. one _____

Skimming

Quickly reread "A Day in the Life of Kotaro Nohmura" and fill in his diary for a typical day. Say where he is or what he's doing.

7:00 A.M. **getting ready for work**	8:00 A.M.
9:00 A.M.	10:00 A.M.
11:00 A.M.	12:00 P.M.
1:00 P.M.	2:00 P.M.
3:00 P.M.	4:00 P.M.
5:00 P.M.	6:00 P.M.
7:00 P.M.	8:00 P.M.
9:00 P.M.	10:00 P.M.
11:00 P.M.	12:00 A.M.

Decide if the statements are true (T) or false (F). Write the sentence from the story that supports your answer. If the article doesn't give the answer, write *It doesn't say.*

EXAMPLE: Kotaro Nohmura works for a computer company. ___*F*___
When Kotaro Nohmura, an executive of an Osaka tent manufacturer, arrives home from work, it is almost midnight.
_____

1. Nohmura's children wake up after 7:30 A.M. _____

_____

2. Nohmura sees his children a lot during the week. _____

_____

3. Nohmura's children are unhappy. _____

_____

4. The Nohmura family has a large apartment. _____

_____

5. Nohmura usually eats a big lunch. _____

_____

6. Nohmura's office is in the same building as the factory. _____

_____

7. Going out to dinner is part of Nohmura's work. _____

_____

8. Nohmura's wife goes to business dinners with him. _____

_____

9. Nohmura would like to come home earlier at night. _____

_____

10. Nohmura works six days a week. _____

_____

4 *Vocabulary*
WORK WITH A PARTNER

**VERBS. Fill in each of the blanks with a verb. Pay close attention to the
form. Use the list at the bottom of the page if you need help.**

When Kotaro Nohmura, an executive of an Osaka tent manufacturer,

_____ home from work, it is almost midnight. He _____ a quick
    1   2

look at his children. They _____ asleep, exactly as they were when he
                                  3

_____ at 7:30 that morning. This _____ usually the only contact
    4   5

Nohmura _____ with his children during the week. Like most Japanese
                   6

executives, his day _____ early and _____ late.
                          7   8

Nohmura _____ $51,000 a year before taxes. He and his family
                   9

_____ in a four-room apartment outside the city of Kobe. Six days a
    10

week, he _____ at 7:00 and _____ a Western-style breakfast
                11   12

prepared by his 32-year-old wife, Sanae. Then he _____ 40 minutes to his
                                                            13

office in a busy section of Osaka.

Nohmura _____ most of his morning at his desk in his tiny office. He
                    14

_____ his small space because he doesn't have to _____ up to get
    15   16

what he needs. There he _____ reports and _____ about tent
                               17   18

designs with engineers. He seldom _____ to business lunches. He usually
                                      19

_____ a quick bowl of noodles at a nearby restaurant.
    20

arrive	earn	get up	leave	spend	take
be	eat	go	like	stand	talk
drive	end	have	live	start	write

37

DOING BUSINESS WITH THE JAPANESE

*S*ome *dos and don'ts*

Business between the United States and Japan is growing. Every week hundreds of American businesspeople fly to Japan and try to sell their company's products there. However, the Japanese way of doing business is quite different from the American way. This can cause problems. Here is some advice for American salespeople to read before they get on the plane to Tokyo.

6 *Scanning*

WORK WITH A PARTNER

DECISION-MAKING. Read the plans of a businesswoman who is going to Japan. Do you think her plans are good for doing business with the Japanese? Check (✔) YES or NO according to the information in the article. Explain your answer.

Business Plans—Japan	YES	NO
1. I'll show that I'm friendly by using first names.		
2. I'll say "Hello," "Goodbye," and "Thank you" in Japanese.		
3. I'll give everyone my business card.		
4. I'll always smile, even if I'm angry.		
5. I'll know everything about my company's product.		

DO

- Be pleasant, polite, friendly, open, responsible, and efficient.
- Speak a little Japanese.
- Use an interpreter when business is serious.

- Bring plenty of business cards.

- Know your facts.

- Try to spend time after work with the businesspeople you meet. Go out to dinner or have drinks with them.
- Learn as much as you can about Japanese history and customs.

WHY?

Japanese people admire these qualities.

Japanese people will appreciate the effort.
Many Japanese businesspeople speak English, but the Japanese and American ways of thinking are very different. It's a good idea to have someone with you who understands the Japanese way.
The Japanese exchange cards more often than Americans.
The Japanese like details and technical information. If you can't answer their questions, you may lose sales.
They may be more interested in doing business with you if you have a friendly relationship.

Japanese people are proud of their culture and appreciate foreigners who try to learn about their country.

DON'T

- Don't be late.
- Don't lose your temper.
- Don't call people by their first names, especially older people.
- Don't expect a clear "No" for an answer.
- Don't expect businesspeople to invite you to their homes.
- Don't act more Japanese than the Japanese.

WHY NOT?

The Japanese expect people to be on time.
The Japanese admire people who can stay calm.
In general, Japanese social behavior is more formal than American behavior.
It isn't polite. Instead, the Japanese will say something like "It's very difficult."
It isn't the Japanese custom to bring business into the home.
This is one of the worst things a foreigner can do in Japan. Use good manners, but act like an American.

	YES	NO
6. I'll expect an answer right away.		
7. I'll invite people for long lunches at a restaurant, to talk about business.		
8. I won't need an interpreter; everyone speaks English.		
9. I'll bow when I meet people; it's a nice Japanese custom.		

7 Vocabulary

GETTING THE MEANING FROM CONTEXT. Look in the box to find the word that completes each of the sentences.

customs	efficient	polite	relationships
decisions	exchange	pressure	technical

1. People in different countries have different _____. For example, in the United States, women usually don't shake hands with other women socially, but at a business meeting they do.

2. At a business conference, people _____ information and new ideas with each other.

3. It's important to be _____ when you travel. Learn to say "Please," "Thank you," and "You're welcome" in other languages.

4. Businesspeople from one company try to have friendly _____ with people from other companies.

5. If you're an engineer, you can understand _____ ideas and vocabulary.

6. Executives are often under a lot of _____. They have to go to meetings and write reports. Many also bring work home at night.

7. Sometimes executives must make very difficult _____. For example, they may have to close a factory, and put people out of work.

8. A good manager doesn't waste time. She uses every minute of the day in the best way possible. She is very _____ and well-organized.

You are going to your partner's country to do business. Interview your partner about "dos and don'ts" there. Are they the same as or different from those in the United States?

Dos and Don'ts	Partner's Country	United States
1. Are people on time for appointments? If not, how late can you be?		
2. Do people talk about business right away? If not, what happens first?		
3. Should I bring a lot of business cards?		
4. Do people talk business during lunches or dinners?		
5. Will I be invited to a business acquaintance's home?		
6. Should I try to speak your language?		
7. What should I never do?		
8. Will I get fast, direct answers from the people that I'm talking to?		
9. Do people in your country think that "time is money"?		
10. Will a woman have trouble doing business in your country?		

If you have other questions, continue asking them!

Is business in your partner's country more like business in the United States or business in Japan? _____

Modern Fathers Have Pleasures

and Problems

CHAPTER 5

Pre-reading

WORK WITH A GROUP

1. Talk about the fathers and children in the pictures. Write down any vocabulary words that are new for you.

   _____

2. What is each father doing?

   a. Picture 1 _____

   b. Picture 2 _____

   c. Picture 3 _____

   d. Picture 4 _____

   Do fathers in your country do these things too?

3. Together, make a list of the things a man should do to be a good father.

4. The next article is "Modern Fathers Have Pleasures and Problems." Check (✔) the things you think this article will talk about.
   - ☐ Fathers in the past
   - ☐ Good and bad things about being a father
   - ☐ Mothers and children
   - ☐ What fathers do at work
   - ☐ Why fathers are doing more at home

Read the article. See whether your guesses are correct. Then compare your list from Exercise 3 with the things that James Hogan and Harlan Swift do. Are these men good fathers?

Modern Fathers Have Pleasures and Problems

James Hogan, 38, became a father 18 months ago. When his daughter was born, he quit his full-time job. He wanted to have more time to spend with his child.

"I wanted to be a real father to my daughter," says Hogan of Washington, D.C.

At first, Hogan had a lot of problems. "I had a lot to learn about babies," he says. "For example, I didn't know how to change a diaper and I wasn't sure how to hold a baby."

There are thousands of fathers like Hogan in the United States today. These "liberated dads" are spending more time with their children—holding them, feeding them, playing with them, and changing their diapers.

There are many reasons for this change. One reason is that modern men have more free time away from work. Another reason is that more married women with children work outside the home. These mothers are too busy to do all the housework and take care of the children alone. Their husbands have to help them.

Modern fathers are enjoying the change. James Hogan spends 25 to 30 hours per week with his daughter. He says he isn't sorry he left his job. "I wanted more time to be with my daughter, and now I have it," he says.

Another father who is enjoying the change is Harlan Swift, a 34-year-old engineer and father of two. "Spending time with the kids is the most important thing in my life. I enjoy every minute I'm with them," Swift says.

Not many men can afford to quit work when they become fathers. They don't have enough money. Combining a full-time job and home life is difficult. You need a lot of energy. As Harlan Swift says, "I never have enough time to do everything."

Modern fathers will need to learn to balance work at home with their jobs outside the home. They will also need to learn new skills. Like James Hogan, many men are uncomfortable holding babies or changing diapers. That is not going to change overnight.

6. A lot of men begin to work part-time v

_____

7. Harlan Swift could use a 26-hour day. _____

_____

8. The author thinks that in a few years n
babies. _____

_____

2. MAKING INFERENCES. Circle *all*
correct. Explain your answers.

ONTEXT. Match the underlined word
the list in the box.

1. James Hogan thinks that
   a) a father should spend a lot of time 'e
   b) fathers are more important than mot
   c) it's difficult to take care of a baby.

experience

2. Harlan Swift
   a) likes being with his children.
   b) doesn't have a lot of energy.
   c) thinks that his job is more importan

3. The author of this article thinks that
   a) modern women are lazy.
   b) many men in the future will work
   c) men today spend more time with th

e time with their children, so they stop
iey can be at home in the afternoons.

t rich. They can't <u>afford</u> to stop

They can do things with their children
women should do.

to <u>balance</u> all the different parts of their
—and still find time to relax.

3 *Finding the Facts*

skills. They don't know how to take

**Answer the following questions with in
Fathers Have Pleasures and Problems**pletes each sentence.

1. What are "liberated dads" doing with
   a. <u>*They're spending more time hold*</u>
      _____ of hard work and good
   b. _____
   c. _____cademic, social, and physical education.
   d. _____

2. Why are fathers doing more with the of their own children with
   a. _____
   b. _____ to care for a sick child.

3. energy   energetically
   noun   adverb

   a. Children have a lot of _____ .

   b. The young couple cleaned their house _____ because their friends were coming for a visit.

4. enjoy   enjoyable
   verb   adjective

   a. Most families _____ taking a vacation in the summer.

   b. Going to the beach is _____ and inexpensive.

⑤ *Further Reading*

WORK WITH A PARTNER

Henry is a newspaper columnist. He gives people advice about their problems. Here are two letters asking for help. Student A will read the letter on this page. Student B will read the letter on the next page.

Helpful Henry

Student A's letter

DEAR HENRY,

We don't know what to do about our daughter. She is twenty-two years old and won't look for a job. She says we have to take care of her for the rest of her life.

She graduated from college last year. Now all she does is eat like an elephant, sleep, read, watch TV, and listen to records.

We asked two doctors for help. They said that there was nothing wrong with her. The police cannot help because she is not a criminal.

What should we do about her? We are not millionaires, and we are tired of . . .

FEEDING AN ELEPHANT

Now ask your partner the following questions about his/her letter.

1. Who is the letter about?
2. What is the problem?
3. What else do you know about the young man?
4. Does the mother dislike her son's girlfriend?
5. What does the mother want her son to do?
6. What advice does she want from Henry?
7. What advice would you give her?

Student B's letter

DEAR HENRY,

I am worried sick about my son. He is eighteen years old and a senior in high school. Yesterday he told me that he wants to marry his girlfriend. She is sixteen.

I want him to get married. But I want him to graduate from high school and go to college first. My son wants to get married right away. He says he is going to quit school and find a full-time job. (Right now he has a part-time job in a supermarket.)

My son's girlfriend is lovely. But they are both too young to get married. I want my son to complete his education first. What should I do?

WORRIED MOTHER

Now ask your partner the following questions about his/her letter.

1. Who is the letter about?
2. What is the problem?
3. What else do you know about the young woman?
4. Who did the parents speak to about their problem?
5. Did they get any help from these people?
6. What advice do they want from Henry?
7. What advice would you give them?

6 *Discussion*
WORK WITH A PARTNER

Talk about the advice you and your partner gave those parents. Do you agree with each other? Would parents in your countries have these problems?

The Language of Gestures

CHAPTER 6

Pre-reading

WORK WITH A GROUP

1. **Look at the illustrations of the gestures. What does each gesture mean in the United States? Is it the same meaning in your country?**
2. **Talk about these and other gestures that you use. Which ones are okay to use in your country, and which ones have a bad meaning? Which ones do only men use? Are any only for women?**

The next article is called "The Language of Gestures." What do you think it will talk about? Read the article.

The Language of Gestures

People are talkative animals. We do a lot of talking—asking, answering, telling, saying. But we do much of our talking without words. We often use a kind of "body language" to show what we think or feel.

This body language is the language of gestures. We point a finger, raise an eyebrow, wave an arm—or move another part of the body—to show what we want to say. In other words, we "talk" with these gestures. And we make hundreds of these gestures in a day.

People all over the world use gestures. In every country, there are gestures that say "Hello" and "Goodbye." However, this does not mean that everyone in the world uses exactly the same body language. We may have some of the same gestures, but different countries have different customs—and different gestures.

Sometimes the same gesture can mean different things in different countries. For example, Saudi Arabians and some other speakers of Arabic say "Come here" with a gesture that most Europeans use to say "Goodbye." They hold up a hand, palm away from the face, and move the fingers up and down.

Because gestures can say different things in different countries, body language can be a problem for travelers. When Soviet leaders visit the United States, they make a common gesture. They hold their hands together over their heads. This is the same gesture that American boxers make when they win a boxing match. But the Russians are not saying "We won" or "We're the greatest!" They are saying "Thank you for the honor you show us."

Sometimes the same gesture does mean the same thing in different countries. However, *when* people use the gesture may be different. Speakers of English say "this tall" by holding a hand out, palm down. This gesture is okay in Latin America—if you are talking about an animal. If Latin Americans are talking about a *person*, they hold their hand out too—but with its edge to the ground. To a Latin American, an Englishman who says "My daughter is this tall"—and makes a gesture to show the height of a cow—is very funny.

Learning words in a new language is not enough. If you want to talk to people who speak a different language, you might have to learn some new gestures too.

1 Skimming

Quickly reread "The Language of Gestures." Write five *general* sentences about gestures, or body language. Don't describe specific gestures.

EXAMPLE: *We can talk without words by using body language.*

1. _____

2. _____

3. _____

4. _____

5. _____

2 Choosing a Different Title
WORK WITH A PARTNER

The title of the last article is "The Language of Gestures." Look at the list of other titles below. Find four that you think are also good. Number them, starting with the one you think is the best.

a) ____ People Talk a Lot
b) ____ Talking Without Words
c) ____ Everyone Should Speak the Same Language
d) ____ Body Language Around the World
e) ____ Gestures in the United States
f) ____ Saying "Goodbye" in Italy
g) ____ Words and Gestures
h) ____ Different Countries, Different Gestures
i) ____ Words Are Not Enough
j) ____ Languages Around the World

What is wrong with the other titles?

Decide if the statements below are true (T) or false (F). Write the sentence from the story that supports your answer. If the article doesn't give the answer, write *It doesn't say*.

EXAMPLE: People often communicate silently. ___*T*___

But we do much of our talking without words. _____

1. People don't use gestures very much. _____

   _____

2. Opening your eyes very wide is a kind of body language. _____

   _____

3. Everyone in the world has the same gesture for "Hello." _____

   _____

4. Italians say "Goodbye" the same way that they say "Hello." _____

   _____

5. Americans and Russians have a gesture that looks the same, but means something different. _____

   _____

6. American boxers put their hands over their heads when they win a fight. _____

   _____

7. Russians are saying "We're better than you" when they put their hands over their heads. _____

   _____

8. English speakers use a gesture for people that Latin Americans use for animals. _____

   _____

4 What Does It Mean?

PRONOUN REFERENCE. Connect the circled pronouns with the words they refer to.

When Soviet leaders visit the United States, (they) make a common gesture. (They) hold (their) hands together over (their) heads. (This) is the same gesture that American boxers make when (they) win a boxing match. But the Russians are not saying " (We) won" or " (We) 're the greatest!" (They) are saying "Thank (you) for the honor (you) show (us) ."

5 Vocabulary

1. WORD FORMS. Choose the form of the word that completes each sentence.

1. customs   customarily
     noun   adverb
   a. In the United States, men _____ shake hands when they meet for the first time. Women usually nod their heads and smile.

   b. Every country has its own _____ .

2. difference   differ
     noun   verb
   a. One _____ between radio and television is that you can see people gesturing on TV. This makes comprehension easier.

   b. The meaning of the same gesture can _____ from one country to another.

3. honors   honorably
    verb   adverb
   a. The soldier fought _____ .

   b. The country _____ important visitors with parades and receptions.

4. talking   talkative
    verb   adjective
   a. Body language is a way of _____ without words.

   b. Some students are too _____ in class.

2. ASSOCIATIONS.   Connect the body part with its movement.   Then demonstrate it.

Body parts

1. finger
2. arm
3. eyebrow
4. eye
5. hands
6. foot
7. mouth
8. shoulders
9. toes
10. nose
11. head

Body movements

a. sniff
b. smile
c. shrug
d. blink
e. clap
f. raise
g. wiggle
h. point
i. wave
j. nod
k. kick

3. RECOGNIZING ANTONYMS.   Find the words in the article that mean the opposite, or almost the opposite, of the words below.

E X A M P L E : line 2   asking *answering*

1. line 1   quiet _____

2. line 4   lower _____

3. line 8   nowhere _____

4. line 13   same _____

5. line 19   unusual _____

6. line 19   separately _____

7. line 22   worst _____

8. line 25   short _____

9. line 29   serious _____

10. line 31   already know _____

Match the descriptions of the gestures with the pictures.

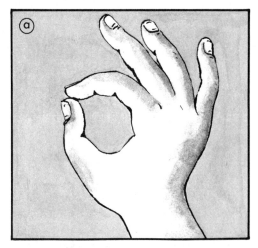

1. In Tibet, people stick out their tongues to say "I respect you." In England, this gesture means the opposite. Children use it to say "I don't respect you."

2. In the U.S.A., people make a circle with the thumb and finger to say "OK" or "All right." In some other countries, however, this gesture means something sexual.

3. In many cities of the world, people shake hands to say "Hello" or "Goodbye." They hold another person's right hand in their right hand and move it up and down.

4. In Russia and England, people clap hands after a play. They are saying "Thank you" to the actors. In Nigeria, however, people clap hands when they meet a person they respect.

5. In Japan, people bow—bend the body and the head—when they meet someone. They are saying "I respect you." In England, actors bow after a play. They are saying "Thank you" to the audience.

6. People in the U.S.A. close the fingers and hold up the thumb of the right hand to say "That's good" or "I like that."

Find out what gestures are common in your partner's country. Your partner will answer the questions *without talking!* Check (✔) if the gesture is the same as or different from what people do in your country.

How do you say . . . ?	Same	Different
1. Yes.		
2. No.		
3. Come here.		
4. Go away!		
5. This tall.		
6. I don't like that.		
7. This is delicious!		
8. This is perfect!		
9. I'm not interested.		
10. I don't care—it's not important.		
11. She's/He's crazy!		
12. Goodbye.		
13. Be quiet!		
14. I want two.		
15. Shame on you! That's bad!		
16. I don't know.		

Some ABC's about Alaska

- 420 beautiful rooms
- Full range of services and shops
- 24-hour coffee shop
- For reservations, call (907) 277-7444

The ANCHORAGE HOTEL

333 Third Avenue
Anchorage, Alaska
99510

CROW CREEK GOLD MINE

Six-hour tour begins with scenic drive to Portage Glacier, then to Mt. Alyeska for chairlift ride to the Skyline Restaurant for lunch. Try your luck panning for gold at Crow Creek Mine and return to Anchorage late afternoon. Crow Creek Tours, Box 1212, Ketchikan, AK 99901. (907) 303-9723.

Salmon Lake Inn

Small inn on private lake. Beautiful rooms. Delicious home cooking. Swimming, water-skiing, sailing, canoeing, horseback riding. Freshwater fishing in lake. Salmon fishing nearby. Write to Box 88, Ketchikan, AK 99901.

Westward Air Service

Sightseeing tours and charters
Box 7, Anchorage, AK 99510

ANNUAL FESTIVAL OF NATIVE ARTS

A weeklong Alaskan culture celebration held in March in Fairbanks. Arts and crafts, traditional singers, dancers, and storytellers. Write to Festival of Native Arts, Fairbanks, AK 99701.

Alaska Discovery

Alaska's oldest, most respected tour company offers wilderness adventures by kayak, canoe, raft, backpack, and skis. Group and individual trips. Experienced Alaskan guides. For information, write: P.O. Box 80VP, Chuglak, AK 99567.

CHAPTER 7

Tongass Forest

25,000 sq. mi. of mountains, glaciers, islands, and forests. Boating, hiking, fishing, hunting, and photography. Fourteen wilderness areas of 5.5 million acres with 151 cabins available for reservation, and ten campgrounds. For information, write BOX 1600, Juneau, AK 99802. (907) 688-7070.

Alaska Luxury Cruises

May through October
Eight Guests Maximum

- King salmon fishing
- Russian history
- Duck/goose hunting
- Eskimo arts and culture

Educational seminars
SEA ALASKA EXCURSIONS
(206) 899-9000

Pre-reading

WORK WITH A GROUP

1. **The title of the next article is "Some ABC's about Alaska." What do you think this article is about? Make a list on the blackboard of the kind of information you think will be in the article.**

2. **What do you already know about Alaska? Are the following statements true or false?**

   a. Alaska is the largest state in the U.S.A. _____

   b. It's always very cold there. _____

   c. Eskimos live there. _____

   d. Alaska was discovered by Englishmen. _____

   e. In the early days, people went to Alaska to find gold. _____

   f. The days are always very short. _____

   g. More than 1 million people live in Alaska. _____

   h. If you go to Alaska, you can speak English. _____

   i. Alaska became part of the United States in 1920. _____

> You have probably found that there is a lot you know about Alaska, but also a lot you don't know. Read "Some ABC's about Alaska." It will tell you many interesting and unusual facts about that state.

Some ABC's about Alaska

Alaska
The name *Alaska* comes from the Eskimo language. It means "great land." Alaska's nickname is "Land of the Midnight Sun."

Anchorage
The financial center is Anchorage, the largest city in the state. It has a population of about 175,000.

Barrow
The most northern point in North America is Barrow. It is an Eskimo town, 330 miles above the Arctic Circle. From May 10 to August 2, the sun does not set in Barrow.

Cost of Living
People recently paid these prices in Anchorage:
Hamburger $2.30–$6.95
Cup of coffee 75¢–$1.50
Public bus fare 75¢
"Alaska" T-shirt $9.00–$12.00
Movie ticket $6.00
Glass of beer $1.00–$2.25

Capital
The capital is Juneau, a small city of 20,000 people.

Discovery
Vitus Bering discovered Alaska in 1741. He was a Danish sea captain who worked for Russia.

Earthquakes
Earthquakes are very common in Alaska. Alaskans often say, "I'll meet you after the afternoon shake."

Eskimos
The first Alaskans were Eskimos. They came to Alaska about 9,000 years ago.

Mountains
Alaska is the home of Mt. McKinley, the highest mountain (20,320 feet) in North America.

Oil
In 1968, oil was discovered in Alaska. "Black gold" helped make the state rich.

Population
In 1980, there were 401,851 people in Alaska. That is the smallest population of any state in the U.S.

Rivers
One of the longest rivers in North America, the Yukon, is in Alaska. It is 1,700 miles long.

Size
Alaska is the largest state in the U.S. —more than 570,000 square miles. It is twice as big as the state of Texas.

Statehood
On January 3, 1949, Alaska became the 49th state of the 50 United States.

Temperature
The temperature in Alaska can vary from −66°F (−54°C)—the coldest in the United States—to 99°F (37°C).

Volcanoes
Katmai National Park is in Alaska. It is the home of the Valley of Ten Thousand Smokes, an area of live volcanoes.

Wildlife
Alaska is the home of the Alaskan brown bear, the Kodiak bear, the fur seal, the caribou, the king crab, and the Alaskan salmon.

Scanning

Read each question. Then look in the box and decide in which CATEGORY the answer belongs. Find the fact in "Some ABC's about Alaska."

```
                        CATEGORIES
Alaska          Discovery       Population    Volcanoes
Barrow          Earthquakes     Size          Wildlife
Cost of Living  Eskimos         Statehood
```

EXAMPLE: How big is Alaska?

Category: _____*Size*_____ Fact: *570,000 square miles*_____

1. What animals can you find in Alaska?

   Category: _____ Fact: _____

2. When did Eskimos come to Alaska?

   Category: _____ Fact: _____

3. How many people were living in Alaska in 1980?

   Category: _____ Fact: _____

4. What does a cup of coffee cost in Alaska?

   Category: _____ Fact: _____

5. When did Alaska become a state?

   Category: _____ Fact: _____

6. Who discovered Alaska?

   Category: _____ Fact: _____

7. Where can you find many volcanoes?

   Category: _____ Fact: _____

8. Why is Barrow a good place for sun lovers in June and July?

   Category: _____ Fact: _____

9. What does *Alaska* mean?

   Category: _____ Fact: _____

Now make up your own questions for the rest of the class to answer.

② Skimming

Alaska is a land of extremes—it has the biggest and the smallest, the most and the least of many things in North America. Quickly reread the article "Some ABC's about Alaska." Use the words in parentheses to find out facts about Alaska. Then write a sentence that gives this information.

E X A M P L E : (highest) *Mt. McKinley is the highest mountain in North America.*

1. (most northern) _____

2. (smallest) _____

3. (longest) _____

4. (largest) _____

5. (second newest) _____

6. (coldest) _____

③ Vocabulary

1. GETTING THE MEANING FROM CONTEXT. Read each sentence. Look in the box to find a definition or synonym for the underlined word in the sentence.

a) another name	d) city where the government meets	g) oil
b) business and money	e) go down	
c) changes	f) number of people	h) saw for the first time

1. _____ In the summer, near the North Pole, the days are very long. In fact, in some places, it's light for 24 hours—the sun doesn't <u>set</u> at all.

2. _____ "Black gold" comes from under the ground like gold, but it isn't a metal. However, it's a very valuable resource because so many people and factories need it.

3. _____ Christopher Columbus <u>discovered</u> America when he sailed there in 1492.

4. _____ In Alaska, the weather is very different in the summer from in the winter. It <u>varies</u> from very hot to freezing cold.

5. _____ Washington is a small city, but it's important because it's the <u>capital</u> of the United States. The President lives there and the legislators make laws there.

6. _____ New York is important as a <u>financial</u> center. The largest banks are in that city.

7. _____ Alaska isn't a crowded state. It has a lot of land but only a small <u>population</u>. In some parts, you can travel all day and not see another person.

8. _____ Sometimes a place or a person has a <u>nickname</u>. For example, Montana is the "Big Sky" state, and a woman named Elizabeth is called Betsy or Liz.

2. WORD FORMS. Choose the form of the word that completes each sentence.

1. discovered   discovery
   verb   noun

   a. Vitus Bering, a Danish sea captain, _____ Alaska in 1741.

   b. His _____ gave the land to Russia.

2. financial   finance
   adjective   verb

   a. Many people _____ a new business by borrowing money from a bank.

   b. Wall Street is the _____ center of the United States.

3. landed   land
   verb   noun

   a. The airplane _____ safely.

   b. In the winter, most of the _____ in Alaska is covered with snow.

4. wild   wilderness
   adjective   noun

   a. Fishermen, hunters, and hikers like to spend time in the Alaskan _____—the parts of the state without towns or cities.

   b. However, they must be careful when they see a _____ animal.

BETWEEN THE WAYS: ALASKAN ESKIMOS TODAY

My name is Gerry Tongass. I am an Alaskan Eskimo. Some people think that all Eskimos live in igloos (snow houses), eat only raw fish, and spend most of their time fishing and hunting. The truth is a little different.

5   There are some Eskimos who live in igloos, but they live in the Canadian Arctic. Most Alaskan Eskimos live in villages and towns. For example, I live in Bethel, a city of about 3,500 people in southwest Alaska. Like most Alaskan Eskimos, I have never seen an igloo—except in pictures. My house is made of wood.

10   Right now, we Alaskan Eskimos are experiencing the biggest change in our long history. We are "between the ways"—the old ways of our people and the new ways of the white people. We used to get all of our food by hunting and fishing. Now we shop for food at the local supermarket. We used to make all of our clothes from animal skins. Now we wear clothes that we buy in department stores. We used to travel by dog sled. Now many of us use snowmobiles.

15   In many ways, our lives are the same as the lives of people in Chicago or Toronto. There are Eskimo bankers, doctors, and hotel owners. We have televisions and VCR's. We sit in chairs, cook on stoves, and sleep in modern beds. We use electricity and oil to heat our homes.

20   However, we have not completely forgotten the old ways. Some of my friends still hunt caribou. Older Eskimos teach young ones traditional songs and dances. Every summer Eskimo families travel hundreds of miles to the places where our ancestors fished. At these ancient fishing places, we fish with a spear— the same way our ancestors fished. While we are at these fishing places, we can feel the spirits of our ancestors. It makes us feel good to be so close to the people 25 and traditions of our past.

5 Finding the Facts

Gerry Tongass says that Eskimos are "between the ways." List some of the old and new ways in Eskimo life.

1. Old Eskimo Ways

   a. _____

   b. _____

   c. _____

   d. _____

2. New Eskimo Ways

   a. _____

   b. _____

   c. _____

   d. _____

6 Choosing a Different Title

WORK WITH A PARTNER

The title of the last article is "Between the Ways: Alaskan Eskimos Today." Look at the list of other titles below. Find four more that you think are also good. Number them, starting with the one you think is the best.

a) _2_ The Truth about Eskimos
b) _5_ Eskimo Ways—Old and New
c) ___ Fishing in Alaska
d) _3_ How Eskimos Used to Live
e) _4_ The History of the Eskimos
f) ___ Modern Eskimo Life
g) _1_ Changes in Eskimo Life
h) ___ An Alaskan Eskimo Speaks Out
i) ___ Dog Sleds and Snowmobiles
j) ___ Eskimo Ancestors

What is wrong with the other titles?

1. TRUE OR FALSE? Decide if the statements below are true (T) or false (F). Write the sentence from the story that supports your answer. If the article doesn't give the answer, write *It doesn't say.*

1. Gerry Tongass lives in a big city. _____

_____

2. The lives of Alaskan Eskimos today are different from 50 years ago. _____

_____

3. Alaskan Eskimos drive cars. _____

_____

4. Modern Eskimos make their own clothing. _____

_____

5. Some Eskimos today go to college. _____

_____

6. Eskimos still remember many of their traditions. _____

_____

7. Caribou are wild animals. _____

_____

8. Gerry Tongass is a woman. _____

_____

2. MAKING INFERENCES. Read each sentence and decide which answer is correct. Explain why.

1. Gerry Tongass's parents lived / didn't live in an igloo.

2. Eskimos eat / don't eat meat.

3. Modern Eskimo teenagers probably wear / don't wear jeans and T-shirts.

4. Gerry Tongass is ashamed of being / proud to be an Eskimo.

Role-Playing

You are a travel agent. Your "client" is planning to take a vacation in Alaska. Ask questions about his/her interests. Check (✔) these answers on the *Alaska Vacation Guide* questionnaire. Your partner's book should be closed while you interview him/her. When you finish, your partner will interview you.

ALASKA VACATION GUIDE

What activities are you interested in as part of your Alaskan vacation?

1. ☐ Staying in the big cities
2. ☐ Staying in small country hotels
3. ☐ Traveling by ship
4. ☐ Camping in state parks
5. ☐ Fishing
6. ☐ Hunting
7. ☐ Seeing wild animals
8. ☐ Backpacking
9. ☐ Boating
10. ☐ Guided tours

11. ☐ Cross-country skiing
12. ☐ Mountain climbing
13. ☐ Looking for gold
14. ☐ Horseback riding
15. ☐ Sightseeing by airplane
16. ☐ Eskimo arts and crafts
17. ☐ Photography
18. ☐ Eskimo music and dance festival
19. ☐ Swimming and waterskiing

Decision-Making

Look at the vacation advertisements on pages 60 and 61. Choose the one that you think your partner would like best. Find out if she or he agrees with your decision.

The TV Is On, But Who Is

Watching?

r false (F).   Write the sentence
f the article doesn't give the

good for family life. ___F___

on on family life. _____

/ision set. _____

_____

York City. _____

_____

e. _____

_____

work. _____

_____

TV are excellent. _____

_____

1. Ta
w ates than listening to music.
vo _____

arefully. _____

2. W _____
Ar
be a meal. _____
wh _____

eir families very much. _____

The _____
Is W
thin ilies. _____

☐ W _____
☐ H
e
☐ W
☐ Tl
☐ Sc
A

Answer each question. Reread the article "The TV Is On, But Who Is Watching?" if you don't remember the information.

1. Why do many people think that television is bad for family life?

    _____

2. What questions did researchers want to answer about Americans' television-viewing habits?

    a. _____

    b. _____

3. What are the five most popular free-time activities in the United States?

    a. _____

    b. _____

    c. _____

    d. _____

    e. _____

4. What do people often do while the TV is on?

    _____

5. What did the researchers learn about Americans?

    _____

    _____

3 *What Does It Mean?*

PRONOUN REFERENCE. Connect the circled pronouns with the words they refer to.

Many people worry about the effects of television on family life in the United

States. (They) say that people spend too much time watching television and that (this)

takes away from more important activities—reading, exercising, talking to family and

friends. But is (this) really true? People in the United States do spend a lot of time
2
in front of (their) television sets. But how much attention do (they) pay to the
3   4
programs that (they) watch? And do (they) spend less time on other free-time
5   6
activities?

Recently, some researchers in New York City tried to find the answers to these
questions. (They) telephoned more than a thousand people all over the United States.
7
(They) asked (them) questions about how (they) spend their free time.
8   9   10

Vocabulary

1. GETTING THE MEANING FROM CONTEXT. Match the underlined word
in each sentence with the definition from the list in the box.

---

a) things to do
b) think about problems; feel troubled
   or anxious
c) related to customs and beliefs that
   come from the past

d) having feelings caused by
   something you didn't expect
e) people who want to learn new facts
   or information

---

1. _____ Many parents <u>worry</u> about the number of hours that their children spend
   watching television. They think that their children won't do their
   homework or get enough exercise.

2. _____ Running and swimming are physical <u>activities</u>. Reading and playing
   chess are mental <u>activities</u>.

3. _____ <u>Researchers</u> have many ways to find out facts. Some work in libraries or
   telephone people. Others work in laboratories and hospitals.

4. _____ Were you <u>surprised</u> to learn that almost every American family has a
   television set, or did you already know it?

5. _____ Many people are losing their <u>traditional</u> ways. They don't wear the same
   type of clothing or eat the same foods that their grandparents did.
   However, they still have the same loving feelings about their families and
   want to spend time with them.

2. DICTIONARY DEFINITIONS. Match the correct meaning with the sentence.

EXAMPLE: *watch* = a) to look at
       b) to look or wait with care and attention

___*b*___ The boy watched for a chance to cross the busy street.
___*a*___ Most people watch television every day.

1. *average* = a) usual, ordinary
      b) the quantity found by dividing the sum of all the quantities by the number of quantities

_____ The *average* of 4, 10, and 13 is 9.
_____ The *average* American child watches cartoons on Saturday morning.

2. *background* = a) the back part of a picture or scene
       b) a person's family, experience, and education

_____ I'm in the front of this photograph, and my house is in the *background*.
_____ The person who interviewed me asked a lot of questions about my *background*.

3. *company* = a) a business
      b) a group of people who are together for social reasons

_____ I don't watch television when I have *company*.
_____ Many soap *companies* advertise on television.

4. *learn* = a) to gain knowledge of a subject by study or experience
     b) to find out, hear about, come to know

_____ When did you *learn* about the airplane accident?
_____ Where did you *learn* English, at home or at school?

5. *popular* = a) liked by most people
      b) common

_____ Rock music and videos are *popular* with teenagers.
_____ It's a *popular* belief that sitting very close to a television set is bad for your eyes.

Further Reading

Researchers studied Americans and found out how they spend their free time.
The left side of the following chart shows their results.

ACTIVITY	PERCENT OF PEOPLE WHO DO IT EVERY DAY	HOW MANY STUDENTS DO IT EVERY DAY?	PERCENT OF CLASS
watch television	72%		
read the newspaper	70%		
listen to music at home	46%		
talk on the telephone to friends or relatives	45%		
exercise or jog	35%		
spend an evening just talking to someone	30%		
read a book	24%		
work at a hobby	23%		
work in the garden	22%		
take a nap	11%		

6 Survey

Take a survey of your own class. Fill in the right side of the chart above with
your results. Then work out an approximate percentage for each activity. For
example, if there are 20 students in class today, and 11 watch TV every day, the
percentage is 50%.

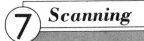

Compare your class with average Americans. Check (✔) the answers to the following questions. Use the information in the chart.

	Your class	Americans
1. Which group watches more TV?	☐	☐
2. Which group reads more newspapers?	☐	☐
3. Who listens to music more?	☐	☐
4. Who talks on the telephone less?	☐	☐
5. Who exercises more?	☐	☐
6. Who spends fewer evenings just talking?	☐	☐
7. Who reads fewer books?	☐	☐
8. Who spends less time at a hobby?	☐	☐
9. Who works in the garden more?	☐	☐
10. Which group takes fewer naps?	☐	☐

Can you give any reasons for your results?

You are a researcher for a television station. Telephone your partner and ask the following questions.

Your partner's book should be closed while you interview him/her. When you finish, your partner will interview you.

1. On an average day, how many hours do you watch television? _____

2. How many hours did you watch yesterday? _____

3. What programs did you watch yesterday? _____

4. What are your three favorite programs—the ones you watch every time they are on the air?

   a. _____

   b. _____

   c. _____

5. Do you agree or disagree with the following statements?

	AGREE	DISAGREE
a. There's too much violence on TV.	_____	_____
b. There's too much sex on TV.	_____	_____
c. There are too many commercials.	_____	_____
d. There are too many news programs.	_____	_____
e. There aren't enough movies.	_____	_____
f. There aren't enough sports programs.	_____	_____

Count the answers of everyone in the class and write the results on the blackboard. What advice can you give to the television-station manager? (For example: "You should have more sports programs.")

Ultralights Are Taking Off

The Quicksilver MX Ultralight

Length: 18 ft. 1 in.

Width: 5 ft. 5 in.

Height: 9 ft. 8 in.

Weight: 239 lbs.

Wing Span: 32 ft.

Body Materials: aluminum, Dacron
plastic, and stainless steel

Maximum Flying Altitude: 10,000 ft.

Fuel Capacity: 5 U.S. gals.

Fuel Economy: 2–3 gph

Maximum Flying Speed: 52 mph

Seating Capacity: 1

Cost: $4,995

Pre-reading

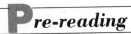

WORK WITH A GROUP

1. The next article is about ultralights, a new kind of airplane. Some people call them "flying bicycles." Look at the picture of an ultralight plane and read the chart describing the Quicksilver MX model. List ten characteristics of an ultralight that make it more like a motorbike than a typical airplane.

a. *It's very small*

b. _____

c. _____

d. _____

e. _____

f. _____

g. _____

h. _____

i. _____

j. _____

2. **Here is a list of some of the abbreviations used in the chart. Match the abbreviation with the complete words.**

1. gph   a. feet
2. gals.   b. inches
3. lbs.   c. pounds
4. U.S.   d. gallons per hour
5. ft.   e. miles per hour
6. in.   f. United States
7. mph   g. gallons
8. $ h. dollars

> Do you think ultralights are popular? Would you like to fly one?
> Answer these questions again after you read the next article, "Ultralights Are Taking Off."

ULTRALIGHTS
ARE TAKING OFF

Across the United States, people are going up in ultralights—low, slow, inexpensive airplanes. Ultralight flying is one of the fastest-growing sports in the country. The first ultralight flight was in 1975. Ten years later, there were more than 25,000 ultralights in the United States.

The United States is not the only country where ultralight flying is popular. There are thousands of ultralights in Australia, Canada, Germany, England, France, and Japan.

Why is ultralight flying so popular? Some people say it is because it is so exciting. "I love the excitement," says Nancy Cooper, an ultralight pilot from Tampa, Florida. "Everything is open around me. I feel like a bird."

Ultralights are also popular because they are cheap. Many people build their own ultralights. They buy the planes in kits—sets of parts to put together. Some kits cost less than $5,000. Flying an ultralight is cheap too. Some ultralights can fly 30 miles (48 kms.) on one gallon (3.785 liters) of gas.

Another reason that ultralights are so popular is that they are easy to fly. An ultralight pilot does not need a license. An ultralight plane does not have to be inspected or registered.

Most ultralight pilots fly for fun. Many of them join ultralight clubs. They attend "fly-ins" on weekends. At the fly-ins, they talk about their ultralights and enter flying contests.

Other ultralight pilots use their planes for work. Farmers use ultralights to look at their land. Scientists use them to study animals they cannot get close to, like sharks. Police use them for patrol work.

Ultralights can be dangerous. Because a pilot's license is not necessary, people can get into an ultralight and fly with no training. Some people have died in ultralight accidents.

For thousands of people, however, the fun is more important than the danger. "Now I can fly for two hours, go a hundred miles, but mostly—have fun!" says Peter Solar of Long Beach, California.

For work or play, ultralights are here to stay.

1 Scanning

WORD GROUPS. Look at the article "Ultralights Are Taking Off." Find the following groups of words.

1. Two states in the United States: _____ and _____

2. Six countries: _____, _____, _____, _____, _____, and _____

3. Four occupations: _____, _____, _____, and _____

4. Five numbers: _____ ultralights, _____ miles, _____ gallon, _____ liters, and _____ hours

2 Comprehension
WORK WITH A PARTNER

MAKING INFERENCES. Decide if the following statements are true (T) or false (F). Underline the sentence in the article that supports your answer.

1. Ultralight flying is a fairly new sport. _____

2. In 1986, there were fewer than 25,000 ultralights in the United States. _____

3. Both men and women fly ultralights. _____

4. Some ultralights cost around $4,000. _____

5. Sharks are dangerous animals. _____

6. You can fly an ultralight on the first day you buy it. _____

7. The author thinks that people will be flying ultralights 50 years from now. _____

83

3 *Finding the Facts*

Answer each question. Reread the article "Ultralights Are Taking Off" if you don't remember the information.

1. What is an ultralight?

   _____

2. Why is ultralight flying so popular?

   a. _____

   b. _____

   c. _____

3. How are ultralights used for work?

   a. _____

   b. _____

   c. _____

4. Why is ultralight flying sometimes dangerous?

   a. _____

   b. _____

4 *What Does It Mean?*

PRONOUN REFERENCE. **Connect the circled pronouns with the words they refer to.**

Ultralights are popular because (they) are cheap. Many people build (their) own ultralights. (They) buy the planes in kits—sets of parts to put together.

Most ultralight pilots fly for fun. Many of (them) join ultralight clubs. (They) attend "fly-ins" on weekends. At the fly-ins, (they) talk about (their) ultralights and enter flying contests.

Other ultralight pilots use (their) planes for work. Farmers use ultralights to look at (their) land. Scientists use (them) to study animals (they) cannot get close to, like sharks. Police use (them) for patrol work.

Vocabulary

1. WORD RELATIONSHIPS. Choose the word that completes each pair.
Explain your answer.

EXAMPLE: *up*:*down* as *in*:___*out*___ a) on b) out c) to d) under
(The colon means "is to" or "is related to.")

1. *low*:*ground* as *high*:_____

   a) earth   b) ocean   c) sky   d) land

2. *driver*:*car* as _____:*airplane*

   a) sailor   b) pilot   c) passenger   d) conductor

3. *expensive*:*inexpensive* as *fast*:_____

   a) popular   b) cheap   c) dangerous   d) slow

4. *flying*:*birds* as *swimming*:_____

   a) fish   b) pilots   c) men   d) horses

2. WORD FORMS. Choose the form of the word that completes each sentence.

1. excitement   excited
   noun   verb
   a. The President's news _____ the country.

   b. You can't imagine the _____ of flying alone for the first time!

2. cheaper   cheaply
   adjective   adverb
   a. Can two people live as _____ as one? People in love think so.

   b. An ultralight is _____ than an airplane, but it's more expensive
   than a motorcycle.

3. inspected   inspection
   verb   noun
   a. The mechanic _____ the airplane before it took off.

   b. Airplanes must pass _____ before they take off.

4. popular   popularity
   adjective   noun
   a. Most radio stations play _____ music.

   b. The _____ of flying as a sport is growing. Many people are
   taking flying lessons and getting their licenses.

Riding the Flying Bicycle

This is flying. I can feel the wind on my face. I am strapped in a bucket seat. There is nothing around me but space. Below me are the brown hills of California and the blue waters
5 of the Pacific Ocean.

I push gently on the left pedal. I move the control stick to the left. My left wing drops and I turn toward the airport. When I see the runway below, I reduce my speed. The engine slows
10 down and becomes quieter. I can hear the wind. The runway moves slowly, up and up, toward me. I come down gently, as in a dream. My wheels touch the ground softly.

I have just made my first solo flight in an
15 ultralight airplane, a miniature flying machine. It is so simple that some people call it "the flying bicycle." Well, it may be simple, but it is more fun than any other plane I know!

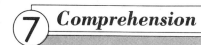

7 Comprehension

Write the correct word on each line. Look at the story for help.

wing	engine
wheel	control stick

① _____

② _____

③ _____

④ _____

Choose the best answer.

1. "Riding the Flying Bicycle" is about
   a) bicycles that can fly.
   b) how to fly a lightweight airplane.
   c) a pilot's first ultralight flight.

2. Paragraph 2 describes
   a) taking off.
   b) landing.
   c) flying over the ocean.

3. Paragraph 3 explains
   a) why the pilot bought an ultralight.
   b) why flying an ultralight is fun.
   c) why ultralights are called "flying bicycles."

9 Ordering

Number the following sentences in their correct order. The first one is done for you.

_____ a. The wind is in my face, and I feel like flying for hours.

_____ b. Now the brown hills of California and the blue waters of the Pacific Ocean are below me.

_____ c. I have just made my first solo flight in an ultralight plane.

___1___ d. I took off an hour ago.

_____ e. I see the runway below and reduce my speed.

_____ f. I push on the left pedal, move the control stick to the left, and my left wheel drops. The plane begins to come down.

_____ g. My wheels touch the ground.

_____ h. But my watch says it's time to return.

10 Vocabulary

RECOGNIZING ANTONYMS. Look at "Riding the Flying Bicycle." Find the words that mean the opposite, or almost the opposite, of the words below.

EXAMPLE: above _below_

1. line 2   unbelted _____
2. line 6   remain still _____
3. line 6   strongly _____
4. line 9   speeds up _____
5. line 10 noisier _____

6. line 12 away from _____
7. line 13 with a loud noise _____
8. line 13 the sky _____
9. line 15 very large _____
10. line 16 complicated _____

11 Problem-Solving

Peter Phillips would like to build an ultralight. However, he wants to be sure that it fits his needs. So he wrote to the manufacturer, Eipper Aircraft.

Underline the questions in Peter's letter. Use the information in the chart on page 80 to answer his questions.

```
                                        115 North Drive
                                        Chicago, Illinois 60609
                                        October 18, 198_

Eipper Aircraft, Inc.
26531 Ynez Road
Temecula, California 92390

Gentlemen:

I am interested in building an ultralight.  However, I
live in a small house and am concerned about parking it.
My garage is 22 feet long by 15 feet wide, and my
driveway is 19 feet long and 9 feet wide with space on
both sides.  Will it fit in both?

I would like to fly from my home in Chicago to my
girlfriend's house in Milwaukee, Wisconsin.  That's
about 75 airmiles.  Can I go nonstop, or will I have to
stop on the way and refuel?  About how much will that trip
cost?  (I'm figuring gas at $1.25 a gallon.)  How long
will it take for me to get there?

One last question:  Can I carry the plane to the airport
on the rack on the roof of my car? It holds about 500 lbs.

Thank you very much for your help.  I'd appreciate
hearing from you soon.

                                        Yours truly,

                                        Peter Phillips
                                        Peter Phillips
```

Have a Good Cry

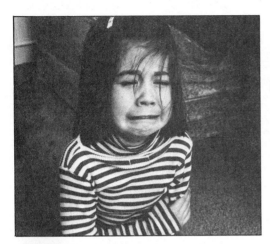

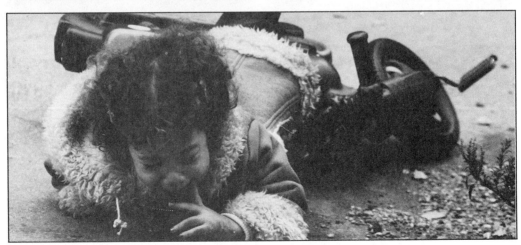

Pre-reading

WORK WITH A GROUP

1. **Look at the people in the pictures. What are they all doing? Write down any vocabulary words that are new for you.**

   _____

2. **Why are they crying? Are they happy or unhappy? Write a reason for each person's tears.**

   a. _____

   b. _____

   c. _____

   d. _____

   e. _____

3. **What do you know about crying? Are the following statements true or false?**

   a. Men cry more than women. _____

   b. All tears are the same. _____

   c. Tears are salty. _____

   d. Crying is good for your health. _____

   e. Crying washes the eyes. _____

Read the next article, "Have a Good Cry." What do you think the title means?

Have a Good Cry

People are the only animals that cry. We cry when we are sad. We cry when we are happy. When someone dies, we cry. When a baby is born, we cry too. We cry for thousands of different reasons. A sunset. A Beethoven symphony. A flat tire.

5   But crying is a mystery. What are tears? How do they come? Why do they come? Modern science does not have all the answers to these questions.

We know a few facts about tears. We know, for example, that all tears have some salt in them. We also know that there are two different kinds of tears—emotional tears and reflex tears. Emotional tears come from feelings, happiness or sadness, for example. Reflex tears are the kind that come when

10   we get a piece of dirt in the eye, or when we peel an onion.

William Frey, a scientist in Minnesota, is studying the chemistry of tears. He collected samples of tears from hundreds of men and women. To make these people cry, he showed them sad, sad films (what some people call "four

15   handkerchief" movies).

Frey's study shows that there is more protein in emotional tears than in reflex tears. But nobody knows why there is this extra protein. And nobody knows where it comes from.

Frey's study also shows that women cry more often than men. In fact,

20   they cry four times as often as men—an average of 5.3 times per month. However, Frey's study does not tell us *why* women cry more. Is it because of biology? Or is it because it is okay for women (but not men) to cry?

Frey has a theory about why people cry, but it is only a theory: he has not proved it yet. Frey says that stress—emotional or physical pressure—

25   produces poison chemicals in the body. Crying removes these poisons and helps people stay healthy.

Psychologists also believe that crying is good for you. They say it helps reduce stress. Stress can cause high blood pressure, heart disease, and other illnesses. Crying can help prevent these illnesses and keep us well. For our

30   health and happiness, it may be good for all of us, men and women, to have a good cry more often.

Scanning

Read each question. Then look at "Have a Good Cry" to find the answer as quickly as possible.

1. The article mentions six numbers. What do they refer to?

   a. line 3: thousands _____

   b. line 8: two _____

   c. line 13: hundreds _____

   d. line 14: four _____

   e. line 20: four _____

   f. line 20: 5.3 _____

2. Where does William Frey live? _____

3. What is he studying? _____

4. What diseases does stress cause? _____ and
_____

② Choosing a Different Title
WORK WITH A PARTNER

The title of the last article is "Have a Good Cry." Look at the list of other titles below. Find five more that you think are also good. Number them, starting with the one you think is best.

a) ___ Why Do We Cry?
b) ___ Tears Are Good for You
c) ___ People Like to Cry
d) ___ Crying Isn't Just for Babies
e) ___ Crying for Your Health
f) ___ People Are Animals
g) ___ Two Kinds of Tears
h) ___ A Crying Experiment
i) ___ Stay Healthy—Cry!
j) ___ Women Cry More

What is wrong with the other titles?

Finding the Main Idea

Reread "Have a Good Cry." Underline the sentence in each paragraph that gives the main idea.

EXAMPLE: *People are the only animals that cry. We cry when we are sad. We cry when we are happy. When someone dies, we cry. When a baby is born, we cry too.* <u>*We cry for thousands of different reasons.*</u> *A sunset. A Beethoven symphony. A flat tire.*

Comprehension

Decide if the statements are true (T) or false (F). Write the sentence from the story that supports your answer. If the article doesn't give the answer, write *It doesn't say*.

EXAMPLE: Cats and dogs can cry.   _*F*_

People are the only animals that cry. _____

1. Science knows everything about crying. _____

_____

2. There are two different kinds of tears. _____

_____

3. We can't stop reflex tears. _____

_____

4. William Frey is a chemist. _____

_____

5. "Four handkerchief" movies are funny. _____

_____

6. Men cry less than women. _____

_____

7. Frey knows why women cry more than men. _____

_____

8. Stress can come from emotional pressure. _____

_____

9. Psychologists think that crying is bad for people. _____

_____

10. People might be healthier if they cried more often. _____

_____

5 Finding the Facts

Answer each question. Reread "Have a Good Cry" if you don't remember the information.

1. When do we cry?

   a. _____

   b. _____

   c. _____

2. What do we know about tears?

   a. _____

   b. _____

   c. _____

3. What does William Frey's study show about tears?

   a. _____

   b. _____

4. How does crying help people stay healthy?

   a. _____

   b. _____

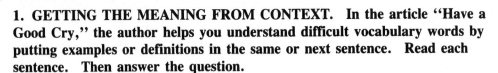

6 Vocabulary

1. GETTING THE MEANING FROM CONTEXT. In the article "Have a Good Cry," the author helps you understand difficult vocabulary words by putting examples or definitions in the same or next sentence. Read each sentence. Then answer the question.

1. line 9: *Emotional* tears come from feelings, happiness or sadness, for example.

   When do you cry *emotional* tears?

   a) at a wedding   b) when you're slicing an onion   c) when you hurt yourself

2. line 5: But crying is a *mystery*. . . . Modern science does not have all the answers to these questions.

   What does *mystery* mean?

   a) something you understand   b) something you don't understand
   c) something you aren't interested in

3. line 10: *Reflex tears* are the·kind that come when we get a piece of dirt in the eye, or when we peel an onion.

   What is true about *reflex tears?*

   a) they come from unhappiness   b) we can't stop them from
   coming   c) they're the same as emotional tears

4. line 14: To make these people cry, he showed them sad, sad movies (what some people call *"four handkerchief"* movies).

   What kind of movies are *"four handkerchief"* movies?

   a) You laugh a lot when you see them.   b) You cry because they show people with serious problems.   c) Horror movies.

5. line 23: Frey has a theory about why people cry, but it is only a *theory:* he has not proved it yet.

   A *theory* is:

   a) an example   b) something that everyone agrees about   c) a scientific explanation that's not 100% sure

6. line 24: Frey says that *stress*—emotional or physical pressure—produces poisons in the body.

   What is true about *stress?*

   a) It's healthy for you.   b) Sometimes it comes when you're unhappy at work.   c) People feel it when they are relaxed.

WORD FORMS

2. Choose the form of the word that completes each sentence.

1. emotion   emotionally

<small>noun   adverb</small>
   a. The man spoke _____ about the political situation in South Africa.

   b. Hate is a very strong _____ .

2. mysterious   mystify

<small>adjective   verb</small>
   a. A good magician can _____ his audience.

   b. Nobody knows why people cry. It is _____ .

3. stressful   stress

<small>adjective   noun</small>
   a. Susan had a _____ day—her boss wanted her to finish a big job in a very short time.

   b. Too much _____ at school or work can make you feel sick.

4. theories   theoretically

<small>noun   adverb</small>
   a. Scientists have many _____ about the beginning of life, but they can't prove any of them.

   b. The scientist spoke _____ about life in the future.

3. Fill in the word-form chart. The forms in Exercise 2 will help you. You may use your dictionary.

NOUN	VERB	ADJECTIVE	ADVERB
		emotional	
	mystify		
stress			
			theoretically

Aggie is a newspaper columnist. She gives people advice about their problems. Here is a letter from someone who is asking for help.

Ask Aggie

Dear Aggie,

What's the best thing to do when a friend starts to cry? The other day I was sitting in a restaurant with my best friend, Betty. She looked sad. Suddenly, she started to cry. She then explained that she and her boyfriend were breaking up. He was going out with another woman.

Tears started to come down Betty's face. I knew she was very upset. I wanted to make her feel better, so I said, "Don't worry, Betty. You'll meet another man soon." But this only made her cry more. I felt terrible!

Aggie, when a friend is physically sick, I know what to do. I'm very good at giving out lemon juice, honey, hot tea, and aspirin. But when a friend has an emotional problem, I feel helpless.

What's your advice? What should I do when a friend starts to cry? What can I do to make a sad friend feel better?

Helpless in Hartford

8 Discussion
WORK WITH A PARTNER

Talk about the answers to these questions.

1. Do you think the letter to Aggie is from a woman or a man? Why?
2. What is the writer's problem? Why is he or she writing to Aggie?
3. What examples does the writer give to show his or her problem?
4. What advice does the writer want from Aggie?
5. What advice would you give the writer?

Ask your partner the questions in the questionnaire. Explain your answers to each other.

CRYING

1. In your country, is it okay for boys to cry? Girls? Men? Women? _____

   _____

2. What do you say to a friend who is crying (or who is unhappy) because:

   a. he was fired from his job? _____

   b. her boyfriend found another woman? _____

   _____

   c. he broke a leg? _____

   d. she came in second in a contest? _____

   _____

   e. he got a ticket for driving too fast? _____

   _____

   f. she won the lottery? _____

   g. his mother died? _____

   h. you spilled hot coffee on her clothing? _____

   _____

   i. he failed an English test? _____

   j. her sister just got married and she wasn't able to go to the wedding?

   _____

3. Do you ever cry? When? Give an example. _____

   _____

ANSWER KEY

Chapter 1

page 3—Scanning

1. 80
2. 1860
3. 12
4. 1927
5. in her seventies
6. 1940
7. more than a hundred
8. more than a thousand
9. six
10. 101

page 3—Finding the Main Idea

1. a
2. b
3. b

page 4—Comprehension

1. F—She had nine brothers and sisters.
2. F—Life was not easy for her as a young girl.
3. T—In 1887, Anna married Thomas Salmon Moses. The marriage lasted until Thomas died in 1927.
4. F—Grandma Moses had no art training.
5. T—She chose these rural subjects to show how Americans used to live.
6. F—He saw some of her paintings in a drugstore window in Hoosick Falls, New York.
7. T—She had more than a hundred exhibitions in the United States and Europe.
8. T—Grandma Moses was simple, honest, and full of life.

page 5—Getting the Meaning from Context

1. upstate
2. training
3. original
4. rural
5. gallery
6. exhibition

page 5—Recognizing Synonyms

1. farmwife
2. world-famous
3. hired girl
4. babies
5. drawing
6. copied
7. childhood
8. exhibition
9. capital
10. full of life

page 6—Scanning

1. North America, South America, Africa, Asia
2. museum, temple, house
3. Flemish, Dutch, French, Italian, British, Spanish
4. gold, silver
5. jewelry, statues, gold, silver, glass, coins, musical instruments, furniture

page 8—Finding the Main Idea

1. b
2. c
3. b
4. c

page 8—What Does It Mean?

1. The Metropolitan Museum of Art
2. 3 million works of art
3. 3 million works of art
4. 3 million works of art
5. Egyptian temple
6. the Egyptians
7. Egyptian temple

Chapter 2

page 11—Pre-Reading

a. not answered
b. F
c. F
d. T
e. F

page 13—Scanning

1. b
2. a
3. b
4. c
5. c

page 13—Finding the Main Idea

1. b
2. a
3. c
4. b

page 14—True or False?

1. T—Koko is a female gorilla.
2. T—Koko knows and uses more than 500 words in sign language.
3. T—In the 1960s, researchers taught chimpanzees to understand and use sign language.
4. F—After only 36 months, Koko could use 184 signs!
5. T—Dr. Francine "Penny" Patterson started to teach sign language to Koko.
6. *It doesn't say.*
7. F—Dr. Patterson, a psychologist, has tested Koko's IQ.
8. F—Koko can understand hundreds of spoken words.
9. *It doesn't say.*
10. F—We have a lot more to learn from her.

page 15—Making Inferences

1. likes—Researchers have to spell out *candy* when Koko is nearby.
2. an adult gorilla—Koko was one year old in 1972.
3. has—Koko can talk about the past or the future.
4. It's difficult—IQ-test questions are written for people, not for gorillas.
5. almost as smart as—Koko's IQ is a little below the IQ of an average child.

page 15—Word Forms

1. a. insults
   b. insulting
2. a. researcher
   b. Research
3. a. speak
   b. spoken
4. a. true
   b. truthfully

page 17—Dictionary Definitions

1. b
   a
2. b
   a
3. b
   a
4. a
   b
5. b
   a
6. a
   b
7. a
   b

page 18—What Does It Mean?

1. Gorilla Foundation
2. Gorilla Foundation
3. Koko
4. Koko
5. Koko
6. Researchers
7. Koko
8. Researchers
9. Researchers
10. candy or gum

Chapter 3

page 21—Pre-Reading

1. No
2. Yes
3. A big turkey dinner
4. Fall
5. Can't answer

page 23—Scanning

1. On the fourth Thursday in November
2. The Pilgrims
3. 102
4. The *Mayflower*
5. 66
6. Plymouth
7. Beans, corn, pumpkins
8. In the fall of 1621
9. Three days
10. Pumpkin pie

page 23—Choosing a Different Title

a, d, e, j

page 24—Finding the Main Idea

1. a
2. c
3. b
4. c
5. c
6. b
7. c
8. a

page 25—True or False?

1. F—The Pilgrims wanted to practice religion in their own way.
2. F—Many Pilgrims became sick.
3. *It doesn't say.*
4. T—Some friendly Indians taught the Pilgrims to plant new vegetables.
5. *It doesn't say.*
6. T—There was plenty of food to eat.
7. T—Friends and families get together for a big dinner.
8. F—In the United States today, Thanksgiving is a lot like the first Thanksgiving in Plymouth.
9. T—For modern Americans, Thanksgiving is also a day for giving thanks for the good things they have enjoyed during the year.

page 26—Making Inferences

1. usually—Some Novembers have five Thursdays.
2. didn't like—The government in England didn't permit the Pilgrims to practice religion in their own way. The king is the head of the government.
3. didn't enjoy—Many people got sick, and many died.
4. More—102 people left England. Some died on the ship. Half of the remaining ones died the first winter.
5. weren't—The Indians taught the Pilgrims how to plant vegetables.
6. colder—The Pilgrims didn't bring enough warm clothing.
7. weren't—The Indians taught the Pilgrims how to plant and hunt.
8. a lot—Friends and families get together for a big dinner.

page 26—Finding the Facts

1. b. The ship was small and crowded.
   c. Many people became sick.
   d. Some people died.
2. a. They didn't have enough warm clothing.
   b. They didn't have enough food.
   c. Half of them died.
3. a. Modern Americans eat the same foods that the Pilgrims ate.
   b. They watch or play games.
   c. They also give thanks for the good things in their lives.

page 27—Getting the Meaning from Context

1. c
2. a
3. b
4. b
5. b

page 28—Word Forms

1. a. celebrate
   b. celebration
2. a. hunt
   b. hunter
3. a. religion
   b. religious
4. a. sailing
   b. sailed

NOUN	VERB	ADJECTIVE	ADVERB
celebrity celebration	celebrate	celebrated	X
hunter	hunt	hunted hunting	X
religion	X	religious	religiously
sailor sail	sail	sailing	X

page 30—Ordering

9	6	1
3	10	2
8	7	4

page 31—Scanning

1. 2 pints (1 liter)
2. Four
3. One
4. Wash them
5. Six to eight minutes

Chapter 4

page 33—Pre-Reading

a. T
b. F
c. T
d. T

page 35—Scanning

1. his daughters' ages
2. his salary
3. the number of days he goes to the office
4. the number of minutes it takes to drive to work
5. the time he leaves his office
6. the cost of dinner in the restaurant
7. the number of courses in the dinner
8. when they left the nightclub
9. the cost of the nightclub bill
10. the number of days he has off

page 35—Skimming

7:00 A.M. getting ready for work	8:00 A.M. driving to work
9:00 A.M. working on reports	10:00 A.M. meeting with engineers
11:00 A.M. finishing reports	12:00 P.M. eating lunch
1:00 P.M. with local client	2:00 P.M. visiting another client
3:00 P.M. at factory	4:00 P.M. back in office
5:00 P.M. getting ready to leave	6:00 P.M. at businessman's club
7:00 P.M. meeting clients	8:00 P.M. taking clients to dinner
9:00 P.M. eating dinner	10:00 P.M. at nightclub
11:00 P.M. driving home	12:00 A.M. drinking tea with my wife

page 36—Comprehension

1. T—They are asleep, exactly as they were when he left at 7:30 that morning.
2. F—This is usually the only contact Nohmura has with his two sons and two daughters during the week.
3. *It doesn't say.*
4. F—He and his family live in a four-room apartment outside the city of Kobe.
5. F—He usually has a quick bowl of noodles at a nearby restaurant.
6. F—In the afternoon, he visits local customers and stops at the factory.
7. T—He usually leaves his office at 5:30, but his work is not finished. . . . After the meeting, he took two important clients to an elegant restaurant.
8. F—When Nohmura returned home, his wife met him at the door.
9. T—Nohmura doesn't like entertaining, but it is an important part of doing business in Japan. (or *It doesn't say*.)
10. T—Sunday is Nohmura's day off.

page 37—Verbs

1. arrives (gets)
2. takes
3. are
4. left
5. is
6. has
7. starts (begins)
8. ends
9. earns (makes)
10. live
11. gets up
12. eats (has)
13. drives
14. spends
15. likes

16. stand
17. writes (reads)
18. talks
19. goes
20. has (eats)

page 38—Decision-Making

1. No
2. Yes
3. Yes
4. Yes
5. Yes
6. No
7. No
8. No
9. No

page 40—Getting the Meaning from Context

1. customs
2. exchange
3. polite
4. relationships
5. technical
6. pressure
7. decisions
8. efficient

Chapter 5

page 45—Scanning

1. b
2. c
3. b
4. a
5. a

page 45—True or False?

1. F—"I had a lot to learn about babies," he says.
2. F—He wanted to have more time to spend with his child.
3. *It doesn't say.*
4. T—More married women with children work outside the home.
5. F—James Hogan spends 25 to 30 hours per week with his daughter.
6. *It doesn't say.*
7. T—As Harlan Swift says, "I never have enough time to do everything."
8. F—That is not going to change overnight.

page 46—Making Inferences

1. a, c
2. a
3. c

page 46—Finding the Facts

1. b. They're spending more time feeding them.
   c. They're spending more time playing with them.
   d. They're spending more time changing their diapers.
2. a. They have more free time away from work.
   b. Their wives work outside the home, and are too busy to take care of the children alone.
3. a. They have to learn to balance work at home with their jobs.
   b. They have to learn childcare skills.

page 47—Getting the Meaning from Context

1. b
2. d
3. c
4. e
5. a

page 47—Word Forms

1. a. combination
   b. combines
2. a. ease
   b. easy
3. a. energy
   b. energetically
4. a. enjoy
   b. enjoyable

pages 48–49—Helpful Henry

Answers for Letter A:
1. It's about the writer's 22-year-old daughter.
2. She won't look for a job.
3. She stays at home all day and sleeps, eats, reads, watches TV, and listens to records.
4. They spoke to two doctors.
5. No. The doctors said there was nothing wrong with her.
6. They want to know what they should do.

Answers for Letter B:
1. It's about the writer's son.
2. He is only 18 years old, and he wants to get married.
3. He has a part-time job in a supermarket.
4. No, she doesn't. She thinks that his girlfriend is lovely.
5. She wants him to complete his education before he gets married.
6. She wants to know what she should do.

Chapter 6

page 53—Skimming

1. Body language is the language of gestures.
2. People all over the world use gestures.
3. Sometimes the same gesture can mean different things in different countries.
4. Body language can be a problem for travelers.
5. If you learn a new language, you might have to learn some new gestures too.

page 53—Choosing a Different Title

b, d, h, i

page 54—Comprehension

1. F—And we make hundreds of these gestures in a day.
2. T—We raise an eyebrow to show what we want to say.
3. F—However, this does not mean that everyone in the world uses exactly the same body language.
4. *It doesn't say.*
5. T—When Soviet leaders visit the United States, they make a common gesture. They hold their hands together over their heads.
6. T—This is the same gesture that American boxers make when they win a boxing match.
7. F—They are saying "Thank you for the honor you show us."
8. T—To a Latin American, an Englishman who says "My daughter is this tall"—and makes a gesture to show the height of a cow—is very funny.

page 55—What Does It Mean?

1. Soviet leaders
2. Soviet leaders
3. Soviet leaders
4. their hands together over their heads
5. American boxers
6. Russians
7. Russians
8. Russians
9. Americans
10. Americans
11. Russians

page 55—Word Forms

1. a. customarily
   b. customs
2. a. difference
   b. differ
3. a. honorably
   b. honors
4. a. talking
   b. talkative

page 56—Associations

1. h
2. f, i
3. f
4. d
5. e
6. k
7. b
8. c
9. g
10. a
11. j

page 56—Recognizing Antonyms

1. talkative
2. raise
3. all over the world
4. different
5. common
6. together
7. greatest
8. tall
9. funny
10. have to learn

pages 57–58

1. c
2. a
3. b
4. e
5. f
6. d

Chapter 7

page 61—Pre-Reading

a. T
b. F
c. T
d. F
e. T
f. F
g. F
h. T
i. F

page 63—Scanning

1. Wildlife—Alaska is the home of the Alaskan brown bear, the Kodiak bear, the fur seal, the caribou, the king crab, and the Alaskan salmon.
2. Eskimos—They came to Alaska about 9,000 years ago.
3. Population—In 1980, there were 401,851 people in Alaska.
4. Cost of Living—It costs from 75¢ to $1.50.
5. Statehood—On January 3, 1949, Alaska became the 49th state.
6. Discovery—Vitus Bering discovered Alaska in 1741.
7. Volcanoes—The Valley of Ten Thousand Smokes is an area of live volcanoes.
8. Barrow—From May 10 to August 2, the sun does not set in Barrow.
9. Alaska—It means "great land."

page 64—Skimming

1. Barrow is the most northern point in North America.
2. Alaska has the smallest population of any state in the U.S.
3. The Yukon is one of the longest rivers in North America.
4. Alaska is the largest state in the U.S.
5. Alaska is the second newest state.
6. The coldest temperatures in the U.S. are in Alaska.

page 64—Getting the Meaning from Context

1. e
2. g
3. h
4. c
5. d
6. b
7. f
8. a

page 65—Word Forms

1. a. discovered
   b. discovery
2. a. finance
   b. financial
3. a. landed
   b. land
4. a. wilderness
   b. wild

page 67—Finding the Facts

Old Eskimo Ways
Eskimos used to live in igloos.
Eskimos used to get all of their food by hunting and fishing.
Eskimos used to make all of their clothes from animal skins.
Eskimos used to travel by dog sled.
Eskimos used to fish with a spear.
Eskimos used to hunt caribou.

New Eskimo Ways
Now Eskimos live in wood houses.
Now Eskimos shop for food at the local supermarket.
Now Eskimos buy clothes in department stores.
Now Eskimos use snowmobiles.
Now Eskimos have televisions and VCR's.
Now Eskimos sit in chairs, cook on stoves, and sleep in modern beds.
Now Eskimos use electricity and oil to heat their homes.

page 67—Choosing a Different Title

a, b, g, h

page 68—True or False?

1. F—I live in Bethel, a city of about 3,500 people.
2. T—We are ''between the ways''—the old ways of our people and the new ways of the white people. (or *It doesn't say.*)
3. *It doesn't say.*
4. F—Now we wear clothes that we buy in department stores.
5. T—There are Eskimo bankers, doctors, and hotel owners.
6. T—Older Eskimos teach young ones traditional songs and dances.
7. T—Some of my friends still hunt caribou.
8. *It doesn't say.*

page 68—Making Inferences

1. didn't live
2. eat
3. wear
4. proud to be

Chapter 8

page 73—Comprehension

1. T—About 98% of American homes have at least one TV set.
2. F—They telephoned more than 1,000 people all over the United States.
3. F—They telephoned more than 1,000 people all over the United States.
4. F—They asked them questions about how they spend their free time.
5. *It doesn't say.*
6. F—Listening to music at home is third. Exercising or jogging is fifth.
7. F—Six out of ten people said that when the TV is on, they seldom pay attention to it.
8. F—During a typical television program, people may eat dinner.
9. F—In fact, people who frequently watch TV read to their children and talk to their families as much as people who seldom watch TV.
10. T— . . . eight out of ten Americans like to spend their free time at home in the company of family and friends.

page 74—Finding the Facts

1. They say TV takes time away from talking to family and friends.
2. a. How much attention do people pay to TV programs?
   b. Do people who watch TV really spend less time on other free-time activities?
3. a. Watching TV
   b. Reading the newspaper
   c. Listening to music at home
   d. Talking on the phone to friends or relatives
   e. Exercising or jogging
4. They eat dinner, do housework, read a newspaper or magazine, or talk or read to their children.
5. They learned that in some ways Americans are very traditional.

page 74—What Does It Mean?

1. watching television
2. television takes time away from more important activities
3. people in the United States
4. people in the United States
5. people in the United States
6. people in the United States
7. researchers in New York City
8. researchers in New York City
9. people all over the United States
10. people all over the United States

page 75—Getting the Meaning from Context

1. b
2. a
3. e
4. d
5. c

page 76—Dictionary Definitions

1. b
   a
2. a
   b
3. b
   a
4. b
   a
5. a
   b

Chapter 9

page 81—Pre-Reading

1. d		5. a
2. g		6. b
3. c		7. e
4. f		8. h

page 83—Word Groups

1. Florida, California
2. United States, Australia, Canada, Germany, England, France, Japan
3. pilot, farmer, scientist, police (officer)
4. 25,000 ultralights
   a hundred/30 miles
   one gallon
   3.785 liters
   two hours

page 83—Making Inferences

1. T—The first ultralight flight was in 1975.
2. F—The first ultralight flight was in 1975. Ten years later, there were more than 25,000 ultralights in the United States.
3. T—Nancy Cooper, an ultralight pilot . . .
   "Now I can fly for two hours . . . " says Peter Solar
4. T—Some kits cost less than $5,000.
5. T—Scientists use them to study animals they cannot get close to, like sharks.
6. T— . . . people can get into an ultralight and fly with no training.
7. T—For work or play, ultralights are here to stay.

page 84—Finding the Facts

1. A low, slow, inexpensive airplane
2. a. It's exciting.
   b. It's cheap.
   c. Ultralights are easy to fly.
3. a. Farmers use them to look at their land.
   b. Scientists use them to study animals they cannot get close to.
   c. Police use them for patrol work.
4. a. An ultralight pilot doesn't need a license.
   b. An ultralight plane doesn't have to be inspected or registered.

page 84—What Does It Mean?

1. people
2. people
3. ultralight pilots
4. ultralight pilots
5. ultralight pilots
6. ultralight pilots
7. Other ultralight pilots
8. Farmers
9. ultralights
10. Scientists
11. ultralights

page 85—Word Relationships

1. c
2. b
3. d
4. a

page 85—Word Forms

1. a. excited
   b. excitement
2. a. cheaply
   b. cheaper
3. a. inspected
   b. inspection
4. a. popular
   b. popularity

page 87—Comprehension

1. engine
2. control stick
3. wing
4. wheel

page 88—Finding the Main Idea

1. c
2. b
3. c

page 88—Ordering

a. 3
b. 2
c. 8
d. 1
e. 6
f. 5
g. 7
h. 4

page 89—Vocabulary

1. strapped
2. move
3. gently
4. slows down
5. quieter
6. toward
7. softly
8. the ground
9. miniature
10. simple

page 89—Problem-Solving

1. Will it fit in both the garage and the driveway?
   Yes, if the wings are closed or removed.
2. Can I fly nonstop from Chicago to Milwaukee?
   Yes. The distance is only 75 miles. The plane carries fuel for 100–150 miles.
3. How much will the trip cost?
   About $3.75 to $5.00.
4. How long will it take to get there?
   About 1½ hours.
5. Can I carry the plane on the roof of my car?
   Yes. The plane weighs only 239 pounds.

Chapter 10

page 91—Pre-Reading

a. F
b. F
c. T
d. T
e. T

page 93—Scanning

1. a. different reasons for crying
   b. different kinds of tears
   c. men and women
   d. handkerchief movies
   e. times
   f. times
2. Minnesota
3. The chemistry of tears
4. High blood pressure, heart disease

page 93—Choosing a Different Title

a, b, d, e, i

page 94—Finding the Main Idea

1. But crying is a mystery.
2. We know a few facts about tears.
3. William Frey, a scientist in Minnesota, is studying the chemistry of tears.
4. Frey's study shows that there is more protein in emotional tears than in reflex tears.
5. Frey's study also shows that women cry more often than men.
7. Frey has a theory about why people cry, but it is only a theory: he hasn't proven it yet.
8. Psychologists also believe that crying is good for you.

page 94—Comprehension

1. F—Modern science does not have all the answers to these questions.
2. T—We also know that there are two different kinds of tears.
3. T—Reflex tears are the kind that come when we get a piece of dirt in the eye, or when we peel an onion.
4. T—William Frey, a scientist in Minnesota, is studying the chemistry of tears.
5. F—To make these people cry, he showed them sad, sad films (what some people call "four handkerchief" movies).
6. T—Frey's study also shows that women cry more often than men.
7. F—Frey's study does not tell us *why* women cry more.
8. T—Frey says that stress—emotional or physical pressure—produces poison chemicals in the body.
9. F—Psychologists also believe that crying is good for you.
10. T—For our health and happiness, it may be good for all of us, men and women, to have a good cry more often.

page 95—Finding the Facts

1. a. We cry when we are happy.
   b. We cry when someone dies.
   c. When a baby is born, we cry too.
2. a. We know that all tears have salt in them.
   b. We know that there are two different kinds of tears.
   c. We know that women cry more often than men.
3. a. There is more protein in emotional tears than in reflex tears.
   b. Women cry more often than men.
4. a. It removes poisons from the body.
   b. It helps reduce stress.

page 96—Getting the Meaning from Context

1. a
2. b
3. b
4. b
5. c
6. b

page 97—Word Forms

1. emotionally
   emotion
2. mystify
   mysterious
3. stressful
   stress
4. theories
   theoretically

NOUN	VERB	ADJECTIVE	ADVERB
emotion	emote	emotional	emotionally
mystery	mystify	mysterious	mysteriously
stress	stress	stressful	stressfully
theory	theorize	theoretical	theoretically